Easy Learning

Data Structures & Algorithms

Java Practice

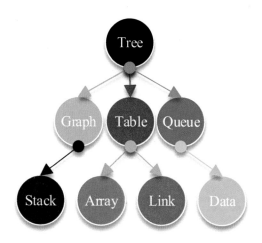

YANG HU

Simple is the beginning of wisdom. learn it easy and well.

http://en.verejava.com

ISBN: 9781096719939

CONTENTS

1. Linear Table Definition 3

2. Linear Table Append 4

3. Linear Table Insert 6

4. Linear Table Delete 8

5. Bubble Sorting Algorithm 10

6. Select Sorting Algorithm 15

7. Insert Sorting Algorithm 21

8. Linear Table Search 25

9. Binary Search 26

10. Single Link 30

    10.1 Create and Initialization 31

    10.2 Add Node 34

    10.3 Insert Node 36

    10.4 Delete Node 39

11. Doubly Linked List 42

    11.1 Create and Initialization 43

    11.2 Add Node 46

    11.3 Insert Node 49

    11.4 Delete Node 52

12. One-way Circular LinkedList 55

    12.1 Initialization and Traversal 57

    12.2 Insert Node 59

    12.3 Delete Node 63

13. Two-way Circular LinkedList 68

    13.1 Initialization and Traversal 70

    13.2 Insert Node 74

    13.3 Delete Node 79

14. Queue 84

15. Stack 91

16. Recursive Algorithm 100

17. Quick Sorting 103

18. Two-way Merge Algorithm 109

19. Binary Search Tree... 112

19.1 Construct a binary search tree.. 112

19.2 Binary search tree In-order traversal............................ 119

19.3 Binary search tree Pre-order traversal.......................... 122

19.4 Binary search tree Post-order traversal 125

19.5 Binary search tree Maximum and minimum...................... 128

19.6 Binary search tree Delete Node 133

20. Binary Heap Sorting 140

21. Hash Table... 161

22. Graph 167

22.1 Directed Graph and Depth-First Search....................... 167

22.2 Directed Graph and Breadth-First Search 175

22.3 Directed Graph Topological Sorting.......................... 183

If you want to learn this book, you must have basic knowledge of Java, you can learn book: << Easy Learning Java>>

https://www.amazon.com/dp/B07Q7MX7Z8

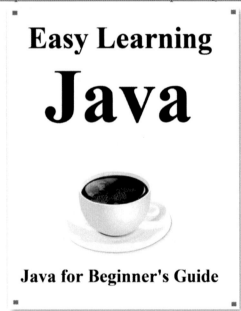

If you already have basic knowledge of Java, skip it, start an exciting journey

Linear Table Definition

Linear Table: A sequence of zero or more data elements. In addition to the first element, each element has only one direct precursor element, and each element has and only one direct successor element except the last one. The relationship between data elements is one-to-one. Linear tables can be represented by one-dimensional arrays.

1. Define a one-dimensional array of student scores

int[] array = { 90, 70, 50, 80, 60, 85 };

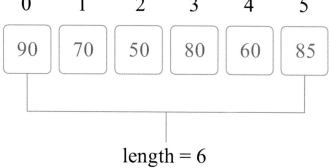

length = 6

Create a test class: TestOneArray.java

```java
public class TestOneArray {

  public static void main(String[] args) {

    int[] array = { 90, 70, 50, 80, 60, 85 };

    for (int i = 0; i < array.length; i++) {
      System.out.print(array[i] + ",");
    }
  }
}
```

Result:
90, 70, 50, 80, 60, 85

Linear Table Append

1. Append 75 to the end of the linear table array.

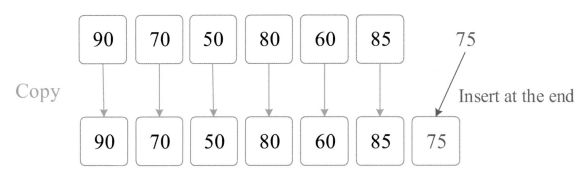

Analysis:
1. Define a original linear table array. The length = 6
2. Create a temporary array(tempArray) larger than original array. length = array.length + 1
3. Copy each value of the original array to tempArray
4. Insert 75 to the last index position of tempArray
5. Finally assign the tempArray pointer to the original array;

Create a test class: **TestOneArrayAdd.java**

```java
public class TestOneArrayAdd {

    public static int[] add(int[] array, int value) { // append value to array
        int[] tempArray = new int[array.length + 1]; // Create a tempArray larger than array

        for (int i = 0; i < array.length; i++) { // Copy value of array to tempArray
            tempArray[i] = array[i];
        }
        tempArray[array.length] = value; // Insert value to the last index of tempArray
        return tempArray;
    }

    public static void main(String[] args) {
        int[] array = { 90, 70, 50, 80, 60, 85 };

        array = add(array, 75); // append 75 to array

        for (int i = 0; i < array.length; i++) {
            System.out.print(array[i] + ",");
        }
    }
}
```

Result:
90, 70, 50, 80, 60, 85, 75,

Linear Table Insert

1. Insert 75 into linear table array at index: i = 2.

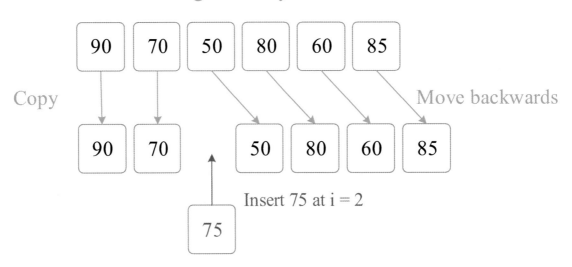

Original Array

Copy

Move backwards

Insert 75 at i = 2

Analysis:
1. Define a original linear table array. The length = 6
2. Create a temporary array(tempArray) larger than original array. length = array.length + 1
3. Copy each value that before i = 2 to tempArray. and then copy remaining elements to tempArray.
4. Insert the 75 to tempArray at i = 2
5. Finally assign the tempArray pointer to the original array;

Create a test class: TestOneArrayInsert.java

```java
public class TestOneArrayInsert {

    public static int[] insert(int[] array, int value, int insertIndex) {
        int[] tempArray = new int[array.length + 1];

        for (int i = 0; i < array.length; i++) {
            if (i < insertIndex) {
                tempArray[i] = array[i]; //Copy value that before i = insertIndex to tempArray
            } else {
                tempArray[i + 1] = array[i]; //Copy remaining elements to tempArray
            }
        }

        tempArray[insertIndex] = value; //Insert value to tempArray.
        return tempArray;
    }

    public static void main(String[] args) {
        int[] array = { 90, 70, 50, 80, 60, 85 };

        array = insert(array, 75, 2); //Insert 75 into array at: i = 2

        for (int i = 0; i < array.length; i++) {
            System.out.print(array[i] + ",");
        }
    }
}
```

Result:
90,70,75,50, 80, 60, 85,

7

Linear Table Delete

1. Remove the value of the index i=2 from linear table array.

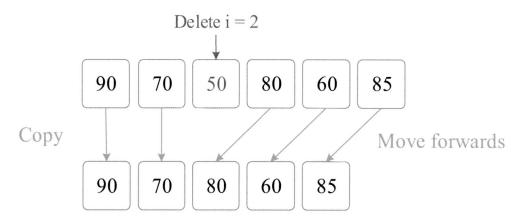

Analysis:

1. Define a original linear table array. The length = 6
2. Create a temporary array(tempArray) smaller than original array. length = array.length - 1
3. Copy the data that before i=2 to tempArray.
Copy the data that after i=2 to tempArray.
4. Assign the tempArray pointer to the original array.

Create a test class: **TestOneArrayRemove.java**

```java
public class TestOneArrayRemove {

    public static int[] remove(int[] array, int index){// remove value from array at index
        int[] tempArray = new int[array.length - 1];

        for (int i = 0; i < array.length; i++) {
            if (i < index) // Copy the data that before i=index to tempArray.
                tempArray[i] = array[i];
            if (i > index)  // Copy the array after i=index to the end of tempArray
                tempArray[i - 1] = array[i];
        }
        return tempArray;
    }

    public static void main(String[] args) {
        int[] array = { 90, 70, 50, 80, 60, 85 };

        array = remove(array, 2); // remove value from array at index=2

        for (int i = 0; i < array.length; i++) {
            System.out.print(array[i] + ",");
        }
    }
}
```

Result:
```
90,70,80,60,85,
```

Advantages of Arrays
1. Arrays represent multiple data items of the same type using a single name.
2. In arrays, the elements can be accessed randomly by using the index number.

Disadvantages of Arrays
1. The number of elements to be stored in an array should be known in advance.
2. An array is a static structure (which means the array is of fixed size). Once declared the size of the array cannot be modified. The memory which is allocated to it cannot be increased or decreased.
3. Insertion and deletion are quite difficult in an array as the elements are stored in consecutive memory locations and the shifting operation is costly.

Bubble Sorting Algorithm

Bubble Sorting Algorithm: Bubble Sort is a sorting algorithm that works by repeatedly swapping the adjacent elements

1. Example: Sort the following numbers from small to large

Compare arrays[j] with arrays[j + 1], if arrays[j] > arrays[j + 1] are exchanged. Remaining elements repeat this process, until sorting is completed.

Illustration.

 No sorting,

 Comparing,

 Already sorted

1. First sorting:

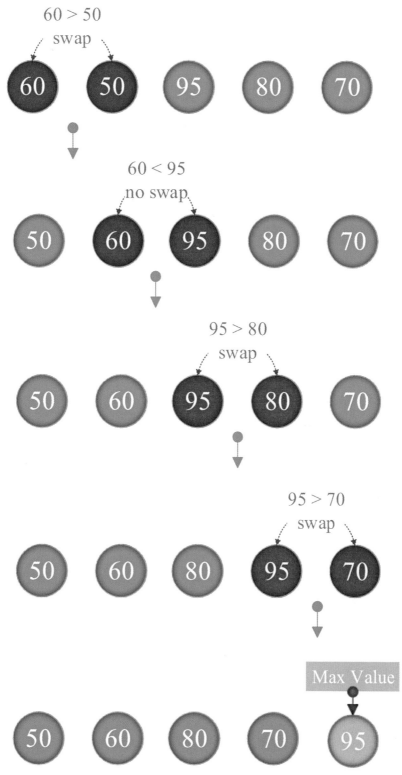

2. Second sorting:

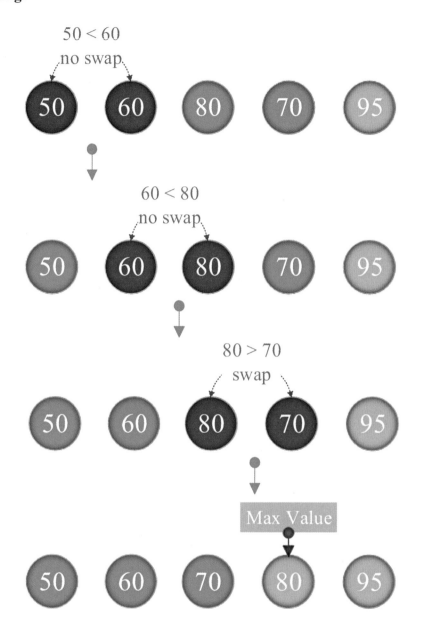

3. Third sorting:

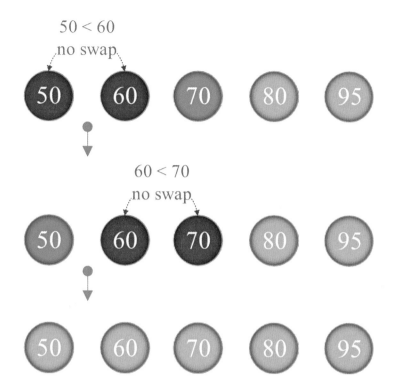

No swap so terminate sorting : we can get the sorting numbers from small to large

Big O notation: describes the complexity of your code using algebraic terms.
$O(n^2)$, which is usually pronounced "Big O squared". The letter "n" here represents the input size, and the function "$g(n) = n^2$" inside the "$O()$" gives us an idea of how complex the algorithm is with respect to the input size.

Big O Notation of Bubble Sorting:
1. Worst and Average Case Time Complexity: $O(n*n)$. Worst case occurs when array is reverse sorted.

   example: (95, 80, 70, 60, 50) -> (50, 60, 70, 80, 95)
2. Best Case Time Complexity: $O(n)$. Best case occurs when array is already sorted
   example: (50, 60, 70, 80, 95) -> (50, 60, 70, 80, 95).
3. Auxiliary Space: $O(1)$ because it only stores one temp value for comparison,

TestBubbleSort.java

```java
public class TestBubbleSort {

    public static void main(String[] args) {
        int[] scores = { 60, 50, 95, 80, 70 };

        sort(scores);

        for (int i = 0; i < scores.length; i++) {
            System.out.print(scores[i] + ",");
        }
    }

    public static void sort(int[] arrays) {
        for (int i = 0; i < arrays.length - 1; i++) {
            boolean isSwap = false;
            for (int j = 0; j < arrays.length - i - 1; j++) {
                if (arrays[j] > arrays[j + 1]) {//swap
                    int temp = arrays[j];
                    arrays[j] = arrays[j + 1];
                    arrays[j + 1] = temp;
                    isSwap = true;
                }
            }

            if(!isSwap) {//No swap so terminate sorting
                break;
            }
        }
    }
}
```

Result:

```
50,60,70,80,95,
```

Select Sorting Algorithm

Select Sorting Algorithm: This sorting algorithm is an in-place comparison-based algorithm in which the array is divided into two parts, the sorted part at the left end and the unsorted part at the right end. Initially, the sorted part is empty and the unsorted part is the entire array. The smallest element is selected from the unsorted array and swapped with the leftmost element, and that element becomes a part of the sorted array. This process continues moving unsorted array boundary by one element to the right.

Sort the following numbers from small to large

Explanation:

No sorting,

Comparing,

Already sorted.

Illustration: 1. First sorting:

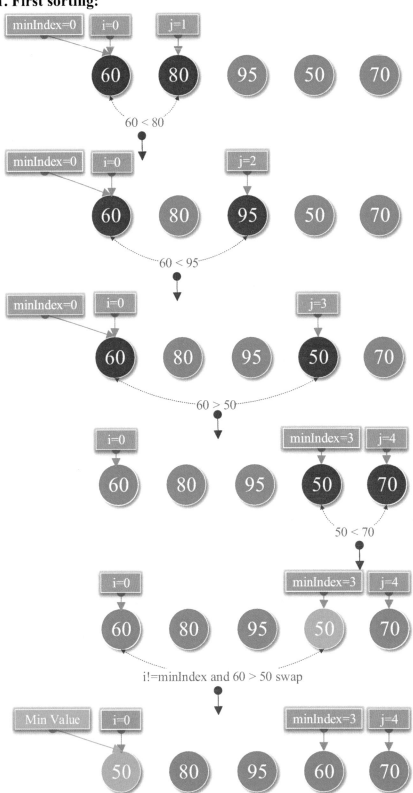

2. Second sorting:

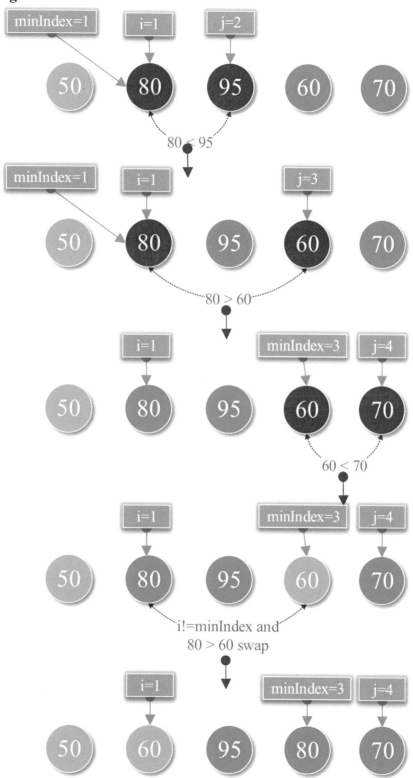

3. Third sorting:

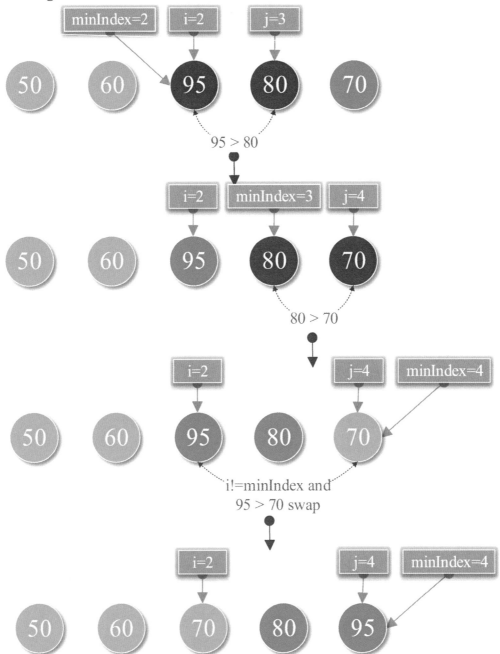

4. Forth sorting:

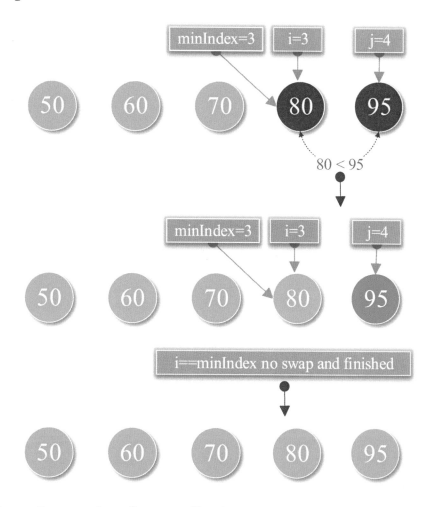

we can get the sorting numbers from small to large

Big O Notation of Select Sorting:
1. Worst and Average Case Time Complexity: O(n*n). Worst case occurs when array is reverse sorted.

   example: (95, 80, 70, 60, 50) -> (50, 60, 70, 80, 95)
2. Best Case Time Complexity: O(n). Best case occurs when array is already sorted

   example: (50, 60, 70, 80, 95) -> (50, 60, 70, 80, 95).
3. Auxiliary Space: O(1)

TestSelectSort.java

```java
public class TestSelectSort {

    public static void main(String[] args) {
        int[] scores = { 60, 80, 95, 50, 70 };
        sort(scores);
        for (int score : scores) {
            System.out.print(score + ",");
        }
    }

    public static void sort(int[] arrays) {

        for (int i = 0; i < arrays.length - 1; i++) {
            int minIndex = i;
            for (int j = i + 1; j < arrays.length; j++) {
                if (arrays[minIndex] > arrays[j]) {
                    minIndex = j;
                }
            }

            if (i != minIndex) //minimum arrays[i] is swaped with the arrays[minIndex]
            {
                int temp = arrays[i];
                arrays[i] = arrays[minIndex];
                arrays[minIndex] = temp;
            }
        }

    }
}
```

Result:
50,60,70,80,95,

Insert Sorting Algorithm

Insert Sorting Algorithm: The first step involves the comparison of the element in question with its adjacent element. And if at every comparison reveals that the element in question can be inserted at a particular position, then space is created for it by shifting the other elements one position to the right and inserting the element at the suitable position.

The above procedure is repeated until all the element in the array is at their apt position.

Sort the following numbers from small to large

Explanation:

 No sorting,

 Inserting,

 Already sorted

Illustration:

1. First sorting:

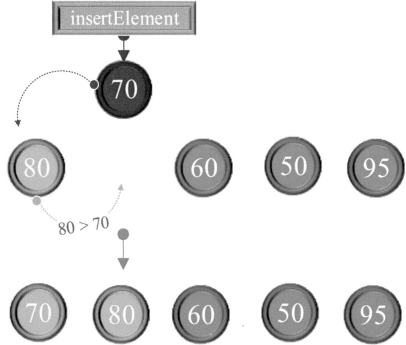

2. Second sorting:

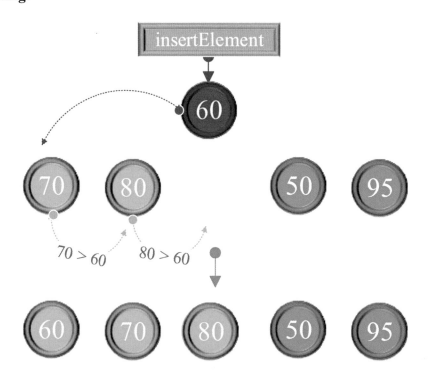

3. Third sorting:

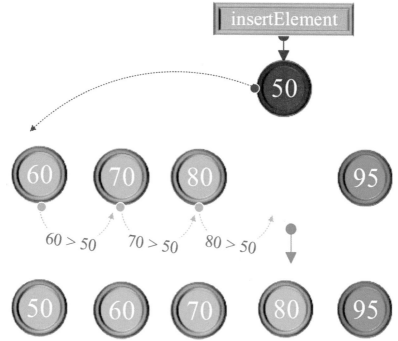

4 Third sorting:

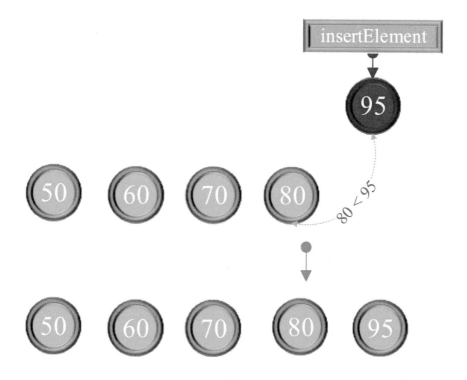

TestInsertSort.java

```java
public class TestInsertSort {

    public static void main(String[] args) {
        int[] scores = { 80, 70, 60, 50, 95};

        sort(scores);

        for (int score : scores) {
            System.out.print(score + ",");
        }
    }

    public static void sort(int[] arrays) {
        for (int i = 1; i < arrays.length; i++) {
            int insertElement = arrays[i];//Take unsorted new elements
            int insertPosition = i;
            for (int j = insertPosition - 1; j >= 0; j--) {
                if (insertElement < arrays[j]) {// insertElement is shifted to the right
                    arrays[j + 1] = arrays[j];
                    insertPosition--;
                }else{
                    break;
                }
            }
            arrays[insertPosition] = insertElement;//Insert the new element
        }
    }
}
```

Result:
50,60,70,80,95,

Big O Notation of Insert Sorting:
1. Worst and Average Case Time Complexity: $O(n*n)$. Worst case occurs when array is reverse sorted.
    example: (95, 80, 70, 60, 50) -> (50, 60, 70, 80, 95)
2. Best Case Time Complexity: $O(n)$. Best case occurs when array is already sorted
    example: (50, 60, 70, 80, 95) -> (50, 60, 70, 80, 95).
3. Auxiliary Space: $O(1)$

Linear Table Search

1. Search linear table array to find : 70 and then return index.

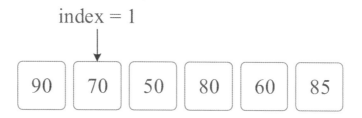

Analysis:

Traverse the value in the array scores, if there is a value equal to the given value like 70, print out the current index

TestOneArraySearch.java

```java
public class TestOneArraySearch {

  public static int search(int[] array, int value){
    for (int i = 0; i < array.length; i++) {
      if (array[i] == value) {
        return i;
      }
    }
    return -1;
  }

  public static void main(String[] args) {
    int[] array = { 90, 70, 50, 80, 60, 85 };

    int index = search(array, 70);

    System.out.println("Found value: 70 the index is: " + index);
  }
}
```

Result:

Found value: 70 the index is: 1

Binary Search

Binary Search:
Divide the data into two halves, determine which half of the key you are looking for, and repeat the above steps until you find the target key.

1. Initialize the lowest index low=0, the highest index high=scores.length-1
2. Find the searchValue of the middle index mid=(low+high)/2 scores[mid]
3. Compare the scores[mid] with searchValue
   If the scores[mid]==searchValue print current mid index,
   If scores[mid]>searchValue that the searchValue will be found between low and mid-1
4. And so on. Repeat step 3 until you find searchValue or low>=high to terminate the loop.

Example 1 : Find the index of searchValue=40 **in the array that has been sorted below.**

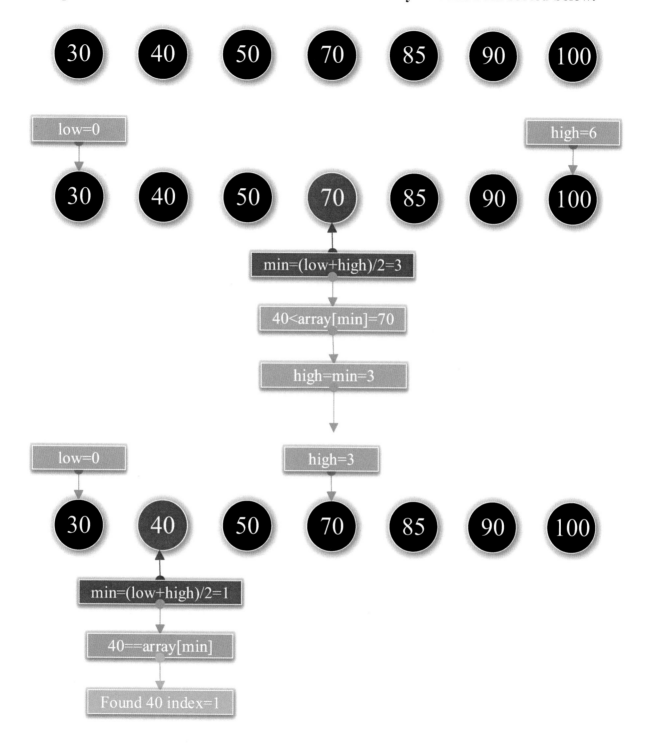

Example 2 : Find the index of searchValue=90 **in the array that has been sorted below.**

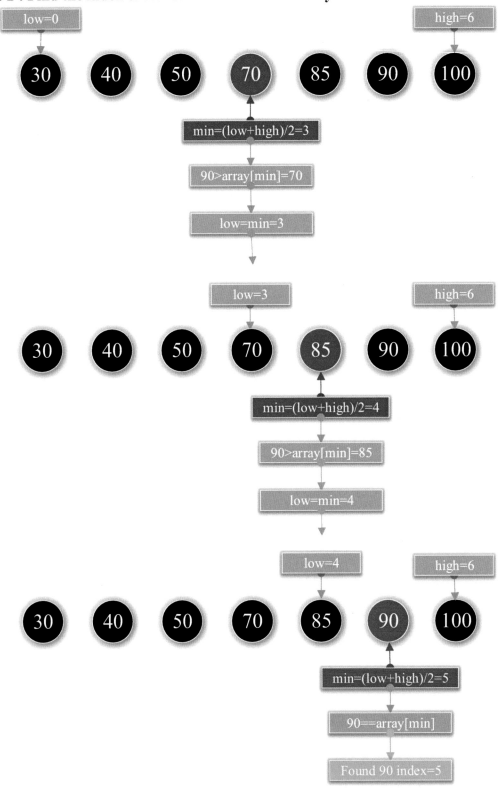

TestBinarySearch.java

```java
public class TestBinarySearch {

    public static int binarySearch(int[] arrays, int searchValue) {
        int low = 0; //lowest index
        int high = arrays.length - 1; // highest index
        int mid = 0; // middle index
        while (low <= high) {
            mid = (low + high) / 2;
            if (arrays[mid] == searchValue) {
                return mid;
            } else if (arrays[mid] < searchValue) {
                low = mid + 1; // continue to find between mid+1 and high
            } else if (arrays[mid] > searchValue) {
                high = mid - 1; // continue to find between low and mid-1
            }
        }
        return -1;
    }

    public static void main(String[] args) {
        int[] scores = { 30, 40, 50, 70, 85, 90, 100 };

        int searchValue = 40;
        int position = binarySearch(scores, searchValue);
        System.out.println(searchValue + " position:" + position);

        System.out.println("----------------------------");

        searchValue = 90;
        position = binarySearch(scores, searchValue);
        System.out.println(searchValue + " position:" + position);
    }
}
```

Result:
40 position:1
----
90 position:5

Single Link

Single Link:

Is a chained storage structure of a linear table, which is connected by a node. Each node consists of data and pointer to the next node.

UML Diagram

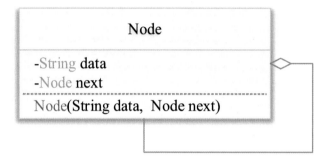

Node.java

```java
public class Node {

    public String data;
    public Node next;

    public Node(String data, Node next) {
        this.data = data;
        this.next = next;
    }
}
```

1. Single Link initialization.

Example : Construct a Single link list

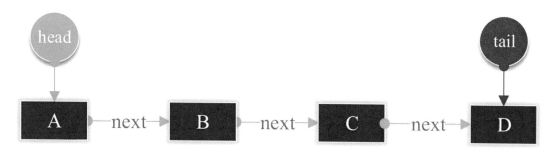

```
public class TestSingleLinkList {

    private static Node head;
    private static Node tail;

    public static Node init() {
        // the first node called head node
        head = new Node("A", null);

        Node nodeB = new Node("B", null);
        head.next = nodeB;

        Node nodeC = new Node("C", null);
        nodeB.next = nodeC;

        // the last node called tail node
        tail = new Node("D", null);
        nodeC.next = tail;

        return head;
    }

}
```

2. traversal output.

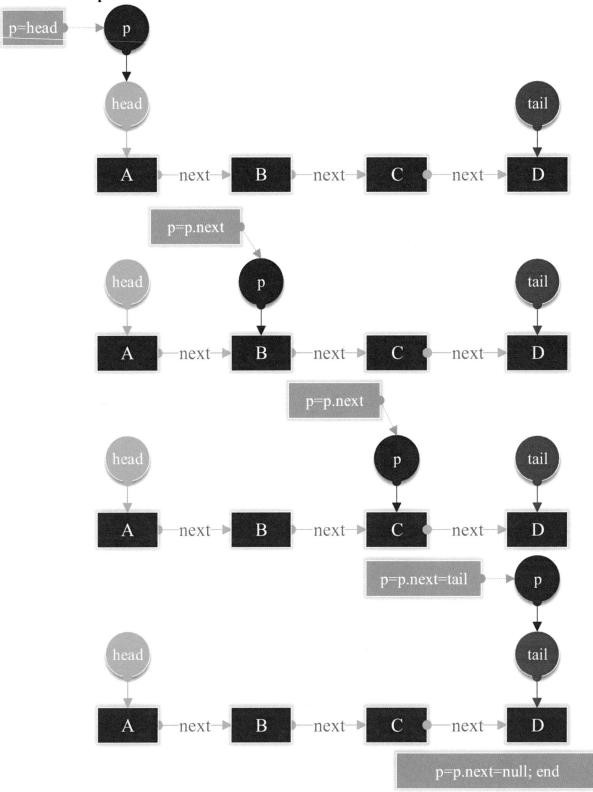

TestSingleLinkList.java

```java
public class TestSingleLinkList {
    private static Node head;
    private static Node tail;

    public static Node init() {
        // the first node called head node
        head = new Node("A", null);

        Node nodeB = new Node("B", null);
        head.next = nodeB;

        Node nodeC = new Node("C", null);
        nodeB.next = nodeC;

        // the last node called tail node
        tail = new Node("D", null);
        nodeC.next = tail;

        return head;
    }

    public static void print() {
        Node p = head;
        while (p != null) // From the beginning to the end
        {
            System.out.print(p.data + " -> ");
            p = p.next;
        }
        System.out.print("End\n\n");
    }

    public static void main(String[] args) {
        init();
        print();
    }
}
```

Result:
A -> B -> C -> D -> End

3. Append a new node name: E to the end.

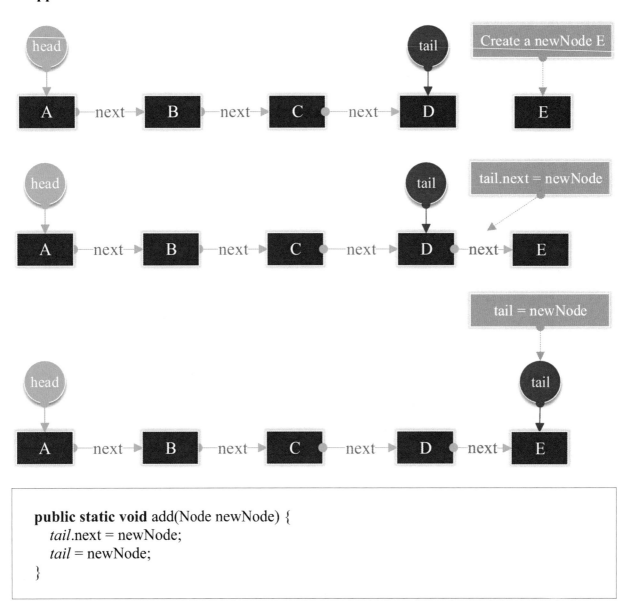

```
public static void add(Node newNode) {
    tail.next = newNode;
    tail = newNode;
}
```

TestSingleLinkList.java

```java
public class TestSingleLinkList {
    private static Node head;
    private static Node tail;

    public static Node init() {
        head = new Node("A", null); // the first node called head node

        Node nodeB = new Node("B", null);
        head.next = nodeB;

        Node nodeC = new Node("C", null);
        nodeB.next = nodeC;

        tail = new Node("D", null); // the last node called tail node
        nodeC.next = tail;

        return head;
    }

    public static void add(Node newNode) {
        tail.next = newNode;
        tail = newNode;
    }

    public static void print() {
        Node p = head;
        while (p != null) {// From the beginning to the end
            System.out.print(p.data + " -> ");
            p = p.next;
        }
        System.out.print("End\n\n");
    }

    public static void main(String[] args) {
        init();
        add(new Node("E", null));
        print();
    }
}
```

Result:

A -> B -> C -> D -> E -> End

3. Insert a node E in position 2.

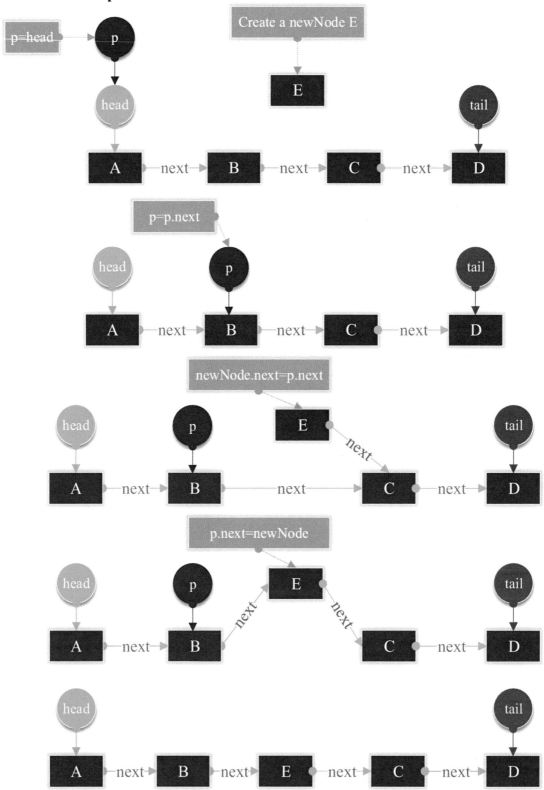

TestSingleLinkList.java

```java
public class TestSingleLinkList {

  private static Node head;
  private static Node tail;

  public static Node init() {
    // the first node called head node
    head = new Node("A", null);

    Node nodeB = new Node("B", null);
    head.next = nodeB;

    Node nodeC = new Node("C", null);
    nodeB.next = nodeC;

    // the last node called tail node
    tail = new Node("D", null);
    nodeC.next = tail;

    return head;
  }

  public static void insert(int insertPosition, Node newNode) {
    Node p = head;
    int i = 0;
    // Move the node to the insertion position
    while (p.next != null && i < insertPosition - 1) {
      p = p.next;
      i++;
    }

    newNode.next = p.next;
    p.next = newNode;
  }
```

```java
public static void print() {
    Node p = head;
    while (p != null) // From the beginning to the end
    {
        System.out.print(p.data + " -> ");
        p = p.next;
    }
    System.out.print("End\n\n");
}

public static void main(String[] args) {
    init();

    insert(2, new Node("E", null)); // Insert a new node E at index = 2

    print();
}
}
```

Result:

A -> B -> E -> C -> D -> End

4. Delete a node at index=2.

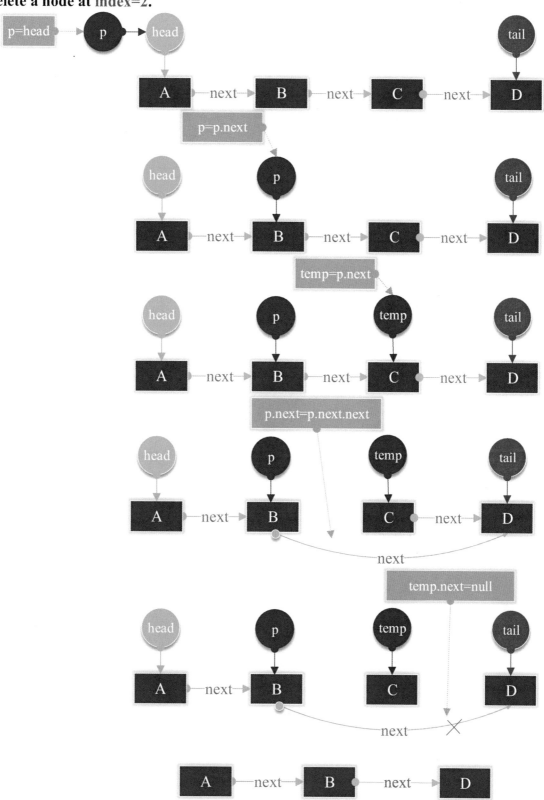

TestSingleLinkList.java

```java
public class TestSingleLinkList {

    private static Node head;
    private static Node tail;

    public static Node init() {
        // the first node called head node
        head = new Node("A", null);

        Node nodeB = new Node("B", null);
        head.next = nodeB;

        Node nodeC = new Node("C", null);
        nodeB.next = nodeC;

        // the last node called tail node
        tail = new Node("D", null);
        nodeC.next = tail;

        return head;
    }

    public static void remove(int removePosition) {
        Node p = head;
        int i = 0;
        // Move the node to the previous node position that want to delete
        while (p.next != null && i < removePosition - 1) {
            p = p.next;
            i++;
        }

        Node temp = p.next;
        p.next = p.next.next;
        temp.next = null;
    }
```

```java
public static void print() {
    Node p = head;
    while (p != null) // From the beginning to the end
    {
        System.out.print(p.data + " -> ");
        p = p.next;
    }
    System.out.print("End\n\n");
}

public static void main(String[] args) {
    init();

    remove(2); // Delete a new node at index = 2

    print();
}
}
```

Result:
A -> B -> D -> End

Advantages of Link List

1. Linked list is a dynamic data structure so it can grow and shrink at runtime by allocating and deallocating memeory. So there is no need to give initial size of linked list.

2. Insertion and deletion of nodes are really easier. Unlike array here we don't have to shift elements after insertion or deletion of an element. In linked list we just have to update the address present in next pointer of a node.

3. As size of linked list can increase or decrease at run time so there is no memory wastage. In case of array there is lot of memory wastage, like if we declare an array of size 10 and store only 6 elements in it then space of 4 elements are wasted.

Disadvantages of Link List

1. More memory is required to store elements in linked list as compared to array. Because in linked list each node contains a pointer and it requires extra memory for itself.

2. Elements or nodes traversal is difficult in linked list. We can not randomly access any element as we do in array by index. For example if we want to access a node at position n then we have to traverse all the nodes before it. So, time required to access a node is large.

Doubly Linked List

Doubly Linked List:
It is a chained storage structure of a linear table. It is connected by nodes in two directions. Each node consists of data, pointing to the previous node and pointing to the next node.

UML Diagram

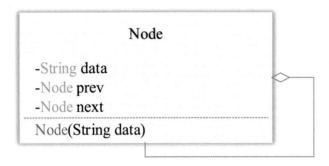

Node.java

```java
class Node {
    private String data;
    public Node prev;
    public Node next;

    public Node(String data) {
        this.data = data;
    }

    public String getData() {
        return data;
    }

    public void setData(String data) {
        this.data = data;
    }
}
```

1. Doubly Linked List initialization.

Example : Construct a Doubly linked list

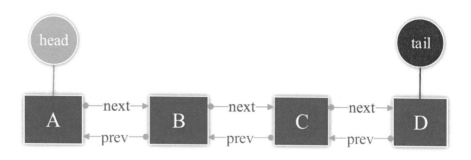

```java
public class TestDoubleLink {
  private static Node head;
  private static Node tail;

  public static void init() {
    head = new Node("A");  //the first node called head node
    head.prev = null;
    head.next = null;

    Node nodeB = new Node("B");
    nodeB.prev = head;
    nodeB.next = null;
    head.next = nodeB;

    Node nodeC = new Node("C");
    nodeC.prev = nodeB;
    nodeC.next = null;
    nodeB.next = nodeC;

    tail = new Node("D"); //the last node called tail node
    tail.prev = nodeC;
    tail.next = null;
    nodeC.next = tail;
  }
}
```

2. traversal output.

TestDoubleLink.java

```java
public class TestDoubleLink {
    private static Node head;
    private static Node tail;

    public static void init() {
        head = new Node("A");   //the first node called head node
        head.prev = null;
        head.next = null;

        Node nodeB = new Node("B");
        nodeB.prev = head;
        nodeB.next = null;
        head.next = nodeB;

        Node nodeC = new Node("C");
        nodeC.prev = nodeB;
        nodeC.next = null;
        nodeB.next = nodeC;

        tail = new Node("D");  //the last node called tail node
        tail.prev = nodeC;
        tail.next = null;
        nodeC.next = tail;
    }
```

```java
public static void print(Node node) {
    Node p = node;
    Node end = null;
    while (p != null) // From the beginning to the end
    {
        String data = p.getData();
        System.out.print(data + " -> ");
        end = p;
        p = p.next;
    }
    System.out.print("End\n");

    p = end;
    while (p != null) // From the end to beginning
    {
        String data = p.getData();
        System.out.print(data + " -> ");
        p = p.prev;
    }
    System.out.print("Start\n\n");
}

public static void main(String[] args) {
    init();
    print(head);
}
}
```

Result:

A -> B -> C -> D -> End

D -> C -> B -> A -> Start

3. add a node E at the end.

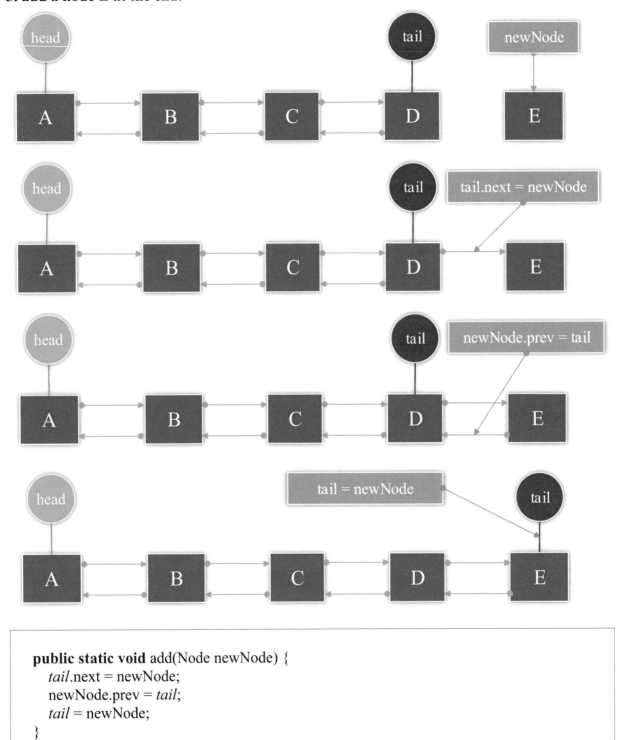

```
public static void add(Node newNode) {
    tail.next = newNode;
    newNode.prev = tail;
    tail = newNode;
}
```

TestDoubleLink.java

```java
public class TestDoubleLink {
  private static Node head;
  private static Node tail;

  public static void init() {
    head = new Node("A");   //the first node called head node
    head.prev = null;
    head.next = null;

    Node nodeB = new Node("B");
    nodeB.prev = head;
    nodeB.next = null;
    head.next = nodeB;

    Node nodeC = new Node("C");
    nodeC.prev = nodeB;
    nodeC.next = null;
    nodeB.next = nodeC;

    tail = new Node("D");   //the last node called tail node
    tail.prev = nodeC;
    tail.next = null;
    nodeC.next = tail;
  }

  public static void add(Node newNode) {
    tail.next = newNode;
    newNode.prev = tail;
    tail = newNode;
  }
}
```

```java
public static void print(Node node) {
    Node p = node;
    Node end = null;
    while (p != null) // From the beginning to the end
    {
        String data = p.getData();
        System.out.print(data + " -> ");
        end = p;
        p = p.next;
    }
    System.out.print("End\n");

    p = end;
    while (p != null) // From the end to beginning
    {
        String data = p.getData();
        System.out.print(data + " -> ");
        p = p.prev;
    }
    System.out.print("Start\n\n");
}

public static void main(String[] args) {
    init();
    add(new Node("E")); //add a node E at the end.
    print(head);
}
}
```

Result:
A -> B -> C -> D -> E -> End

E -> D -> C -> B -> A -> Start

3. Insert a node E in index = 2.

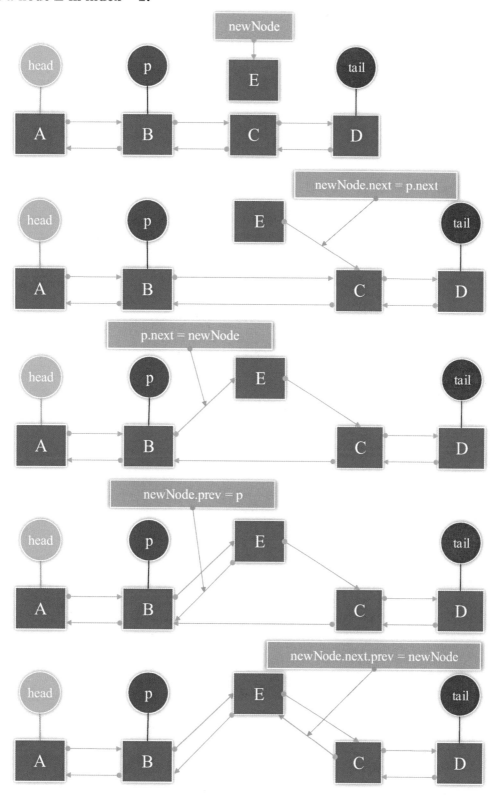

TestDoubleLink.java

```java
public class TestDoubleLink {
  private static Node head;
  private static Node tail;

  public static void init() {
    head = new Node("A");  //the first node called head node
    head.prev = null;
    head.next = null;

    Node nodeB = new Node("B");
    nodeB.prev = head;
    nodeB.next = null;
    head.next = nodeB;

    Node nodeC = new Node("C");
    nodeC.prev = nodeB;
    nodeC.next = null;
    nodeB.next = nodeC;

    tail = new Node("D"); //the last node called tail node
    tail.prev = nodeC;
    tail.next = null;
    nodeC.next = tail;
  }

  public static void insert(int insertPosition, Node newNode) {
    Node p = head;
    int i = 0;
    // Move the node to the insertion position
    while (p.next != null && i < insertPosition-1) {
      p = p.next;
      i++;
    }

    newNode.next = p.next;
    p.next = newNode;
    newNode.prev = p;
    newNode.next.prev = newNode;
  }
```

```java
public static void print(Node node) {
    Node p = node;
    Node end = null;
    while (p != null) // From the beginning to the end
    {
        String data = p.getData();
        System.out.print(data + " -> ");
        end = p;
        p = p.next;
    }
    System.out.print("End\n");

    p = end;
    while (p != null) // From the end to beginning
    {
        String data = p.getData();
        System.out.print(data + " -> ");
        p = p.prev;
    }
    System.out.print("Start\n\n");
}

public static void main(String[] args) {
    init();
    insert(2, new Node("E")); // Insert a node E in index = 2.
    print(head);
}
}
```

Result:
A -> B -> E -> C -> D -> End
D -> C -> E -> B -> A -> Start

4. Delete the node at index=2.

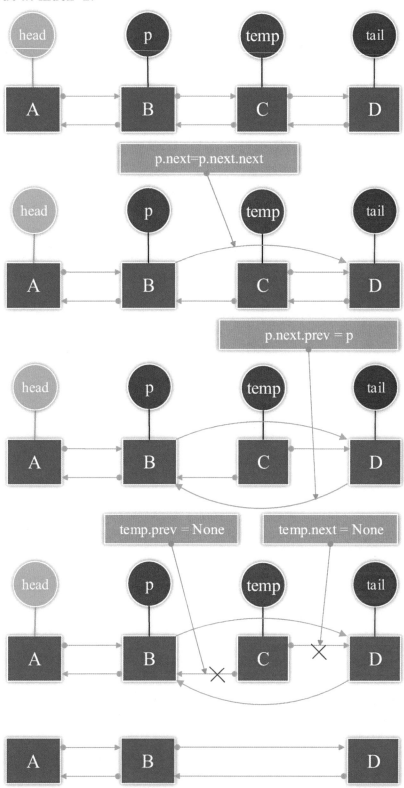

TestDoubleLink.java

```java
public class TestDoubleLink {
  private static Node head;
  private static Node tail;

  public static void init() {
    head = new Node("A");   //the first node called head node
    head.prev = null;
    head.next = null;

    Node nodeB = new Node("B");
    nodeB.prev = head;
    nodeB.next = null;
    head.next = nodeB;

    Node nodeC = new Node("C");
    nodeC.prev = nodeB;
    nodeC.next = null;
    nodeB.next = nodeC;

    tail = new Node("D");  //the last node called tail node
    tail.prev = nodeC;
    tail.next = null;
    nodeC.next = tail;
  }

  public static void remove(int removePosition) {
    Node p = head;
    int i = 0;
    // Move the node to the previous node  that want to delete
    while (p.next != null && i < removePosition - 1) {
      p = p.next;
      i++;
    }
    Node temp = p.next;// Save the node you want to delete
    p.next = p.next.next;
    p.next.prev = p;
    temp.next = null;// Set the delete node next to null
    temp.prev = null;// Set the delete node prev to null
  }
```

```java
public static void print(Node node) {
    Node p = node;
    Node end = null;
    while (p != null) // From the beginning to the end
    {
        String data = p.getData();
        System.out.print(data + " -> ");
        end = p;
        p = p.next;
    }
    System.out.print("End\n");

    p = end;
    while (p != null) // From the end to beginning
    {
        String data = p.getData();
        System.out.print(data + " -> ");
        p = p.prev;
    }
    System.out.print("Start\n\n");
}

public static void main(String[] args) {
    init();
    remove(2); // Delete the node at index=2.
    print(head);
}
}
```

Result:
A -> B -> D -> End
D -> B -> A -> Start

One-way Circular LinkedList

One-way Circular List:

It is a chain storage structure of a linear table, which is connected to form a ring, and each node is composed of data and a pointer to next.

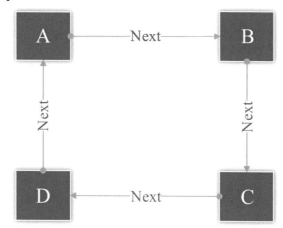

UML Diagram

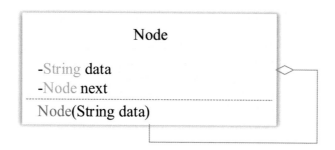

Node.java

```java
public class Node {
    private String data;
    public Node next;

    public Node(String data) {
        this.data = data;
    }

    public String getData() {
        return data;
    }
    public void setData(String data) {
        this.data = data;
    }
}
```

1. One-way Circular Linked List initialization.

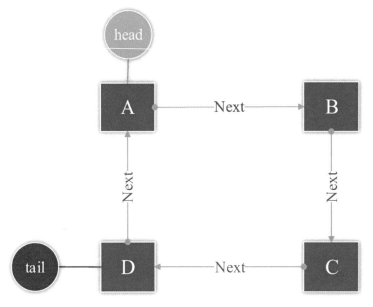

```
public class TestSingleCircleLink {
    private static Node head;
    private static Node tail;

    public static void init() {
        head = new Node("A");// the first node called head node
        head.next = null;

        Node nodeB = new Node("B");
        nodeB.next = null;
        head.next = nodeB;

        Node nodeC = new Node("C");
        nodeC.next = null;
        nodeB.next = nodeC;

        tail = new Node("D");// the last node called tail node
        tail.next = head;
        nodeC.next = tail;
    }
}
```

2. One-way Circular Linked List traversal output.

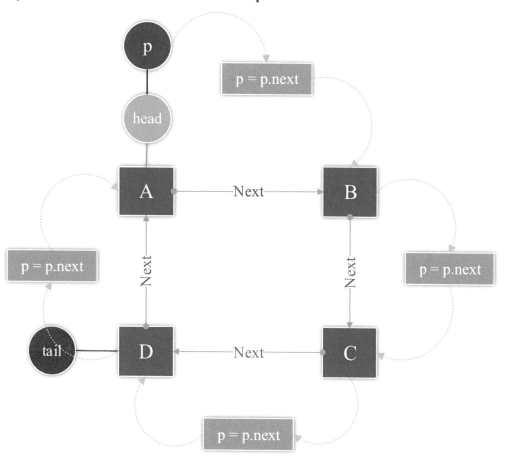

```
public static void print() {
    Node p = head;
    do{
        String data = p.getData();
        System.out.print(data + " -> ");
        p = p.next;
    }while(p!=head);

    String data = p.getData();
    System.out.print(data + "\n\n");
}
```

TestSingleCircleLink.java

```java
public class TestSingleCircleLink {
    private static Node head;
    private static Node tail;

    public static void init() {
        head = new Node("A");// the first node called head node
        head.next = null;

        Node nodeB = new Node("B");
        nodeB.next = null;
        head.next = nodeB;

        Node nodeC = new Node("C");
        nodeC.next = null;
        nodeB.next = nodeC;

        tail = new Node("D");// the last node called tail node
        tail.next = head;
        nodeC.next = tail;
    }

    public static void print() {
        Node p = head;
        do{
            String data = p.getData();
            System.out.print(data + " -> ");
            p = p.next;
        }while(p!=head);

        String data = p.getData();
        System.out.print(data + "\n\n");
    }

    public static void main(String[] args) {

        init();
        print();
    }
}
```

Result:
A -> B -> C -> D -> A

3. Insert a node E in position 2.

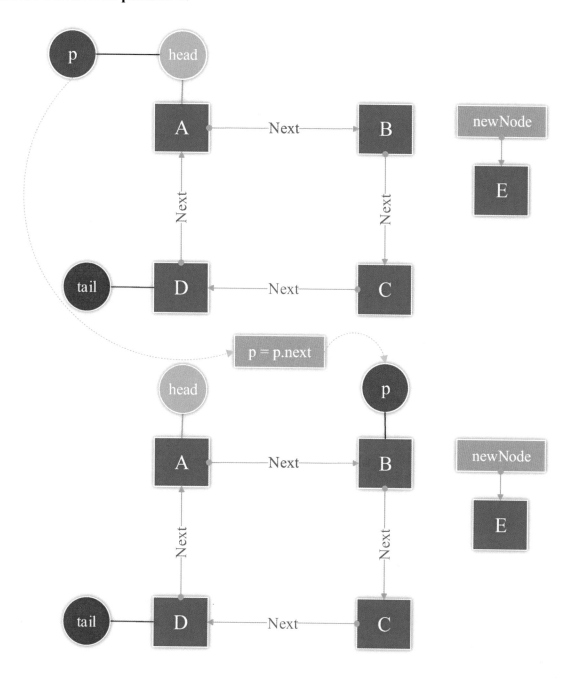

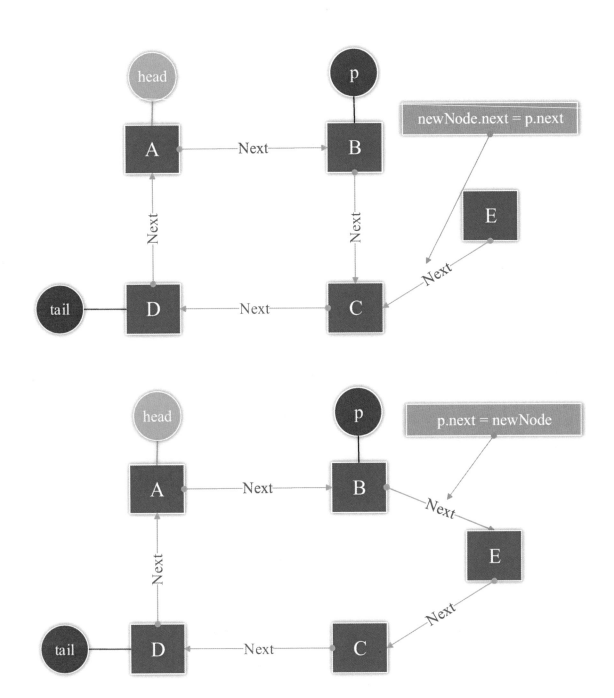

TestSingleCircleLink.java

```java
public class TestSingleCircleLink {

  private static Node head;
  private static Node tail;

  public static void init() {

    // the first node called head node
    head = new Node("A");
    head.next = null;

    Node nodeB = new Node("B");
    nodeB.next = null;
    head.next = nodeB;

    Node nodeC = new Node("C");
    nodeC.next = null;
    nodeB.next = nodeC;

    // the last node called tail node
    tail = new Node("D");
    tail.next = head;
    nodeC.next = tail;
  }

  public static void insert(int insertPosition, Node newNode) {
    Node p = head;
    int i = 0;
    // Move the node to the insertion position
    while (p.next != null && i < insertPosition - 1) {
      p = p.next;
      i++;
    }

    newNode.next = p.next;
    p.next = newNode;
  }
```

```
public static void print() {
    Node p = head;
    do {
        String data = p.getData();
        System.out.print(data + " -> ");
        p = p.next;
    } while (p != head);

    String data = p.getData();
    System.out.print(data + "\n\n");
}

public static void main(String[] args) {
    init();
    insert(2,new Node("E"));
    print();
}
}
```

Result:
A -> B -> E -> C -> D -> A

4. Delete the node at index=2.

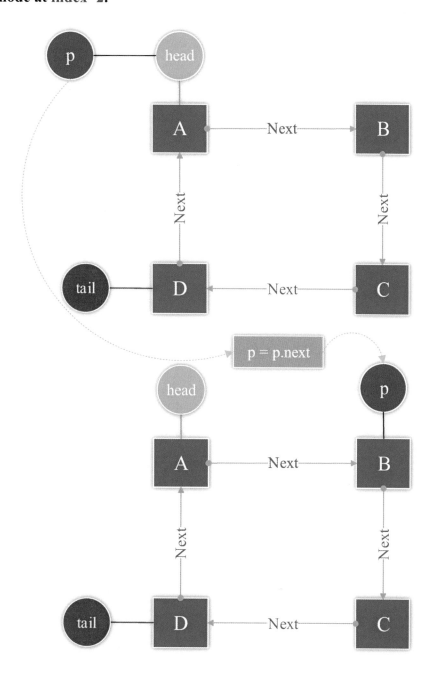

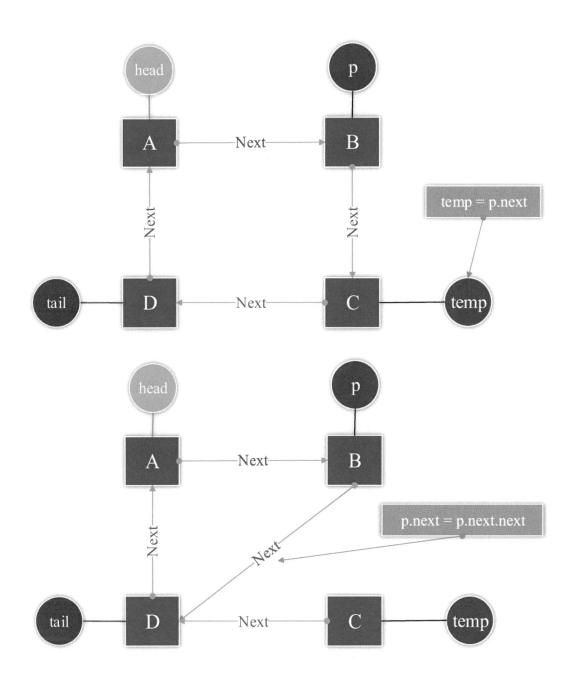

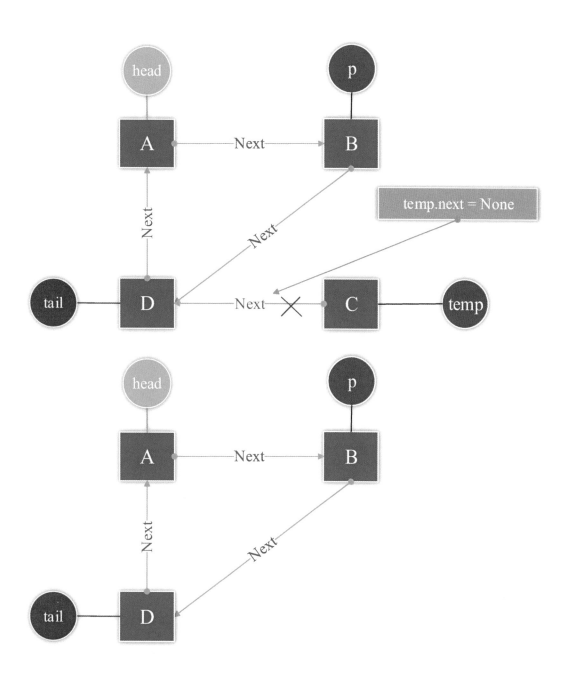

TestSingleCircleLink.java

```java
public class TestSingleCircleLink {

    private static Node head;
    private static Node tail;

    public static void init() {

        // the first node called head node
        head = new Node("A");
        head.next = null;

        Node nodeB = new Node("B");
        nodeB.next = null;
        head.next = nodeB;

        Node nodeC = new Node("C");
        nodeC.next = null;
        nodeB.next = nodeC;

        // the last node called tail node
        tail = new Node("D");
        tail.next = head;
        nodeC.next = tail;
    }

    public static void remove(int removePosition) {
        Node p = head;
        int i = 0;
        // Move the node to the previous node  that want to delete
        while (p.next != null && i < removePosition - 1) {
            p = p.next;
            i++;
        }

        Node temp = p.next;
        p.next = p.next.next;
        temp.next = null;
    }
```

```java
    public static void print() {
        Node p = head;
        do {
            String data = p.getData();
            System.out.print(data + " -> ");
            p = p.next;
        } while (p != head);

        String data = p.getData();
        System.out.print(data + "\n\n");
    }

    public static void main(String[] args) {
        init();
        remove(2);
        print();
    }
}
```

Result:
A -> B -> D -> A

Two-way Circular LinkedList

Two-way Circular List: It is a chain storage structure of a linear table. The nodes are connected in series by two directions, and is connected to form a ring. Each node is composed of data, pointing to the previous node prev and pointing to the next node next.

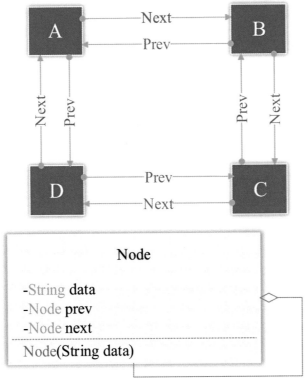

Node.java

```java
class Node {
    private String data;
    public Node prev;
    public Node next;

    public Node(String data) {
        this.data = data;
    }
    public String getData() {
        return data;
    }
    public void setData(String data) {
        this.data = data;
    }
}
```

1. Two-way Circular Linked List initialization

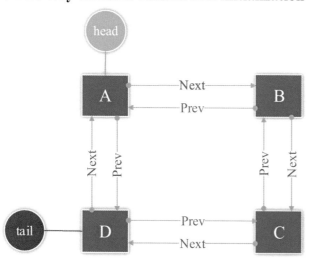

```
public class TestDoubleCircleLink {
  private static Node head;
  private static Node tail;

  public static void init() {
    head = new Node("A"); // the first node called head node
    head.next = null;
    head.prev = null;

    Node nodeB = new Node("B");
    nodeB.next = null;
    nodeB.prev = head;
    head.next = nodeB;

    Node nodeC = new Node("C");
    nodeC.next = null;
    nodeC.prev = nodeB;
    nodeB.next = nodeC;

    tail = new Node("D"); // the last node called tail node
    tail.next = head;
    tail.prev = nodeC;
    nodeC.next = tail;
    head.prev = tail;
  }
}
```

2. Two-way Circular Linked List traversal output.

Traverse from the head by next:

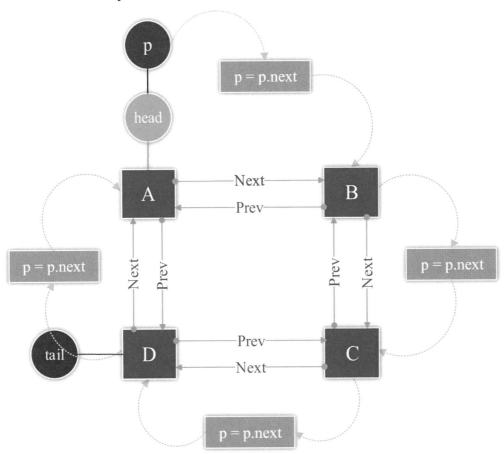

Traverse from the tail by prev:

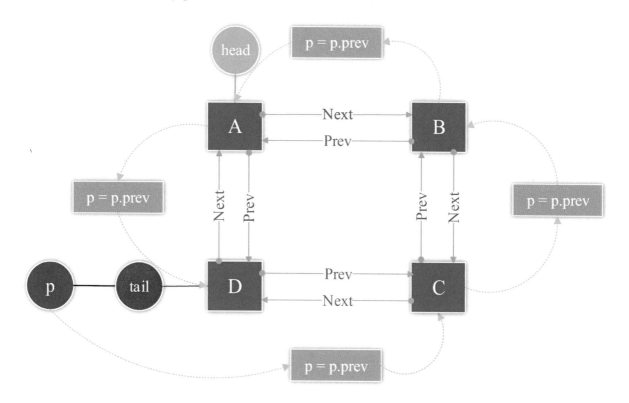

TestDoubleCircleLink.java

```java
public class TestDoubleCircleLink {

    private static Node head;
    private static Node tail;

    public static void init() {

        // the first node called head node
        head = new Node("A");
        head.next = null;
        head.prev = null;

        Node nodeB = new Node("B");
        nodeB.next = null;
        nodeB.prev = head;
        head.next = nodeB;

        Node nodeC = new Node("C");
        nodeC.next = null;
        nodeC.prev = nodeB;
        nodeB.next = nodeC;

        // the last node called tail node
        tail = new Node("D");
        tail.next = head;
        tail.prev = nodeC;
        nodeC.next = tail;
        head.prev = tail;
    }
```

```
public static void print() {
    Node p = head;
    do { // From the beginning to the end
        String data = p.getData();
        System.out.print(data + " -> ");
        p = p.next;
    } while (p != head);

    String data = p.getData();
    System.out.print(data + "\n\n");

    p = tail;
    do { // From the end to beginning
        data = p.getData();
        System.out.print(data + " -> ");
        p = p.prev;
    } while (p != tail);

    data = p.getData();
    System.out.print(data + "\n\n");
}

public static void main(String[] args) {
    init();
    print();
}
}
```

Result:

A -> B -> C -> D -> A

D -> C -> B -> A -> D

3. Insert a node E in position 2.

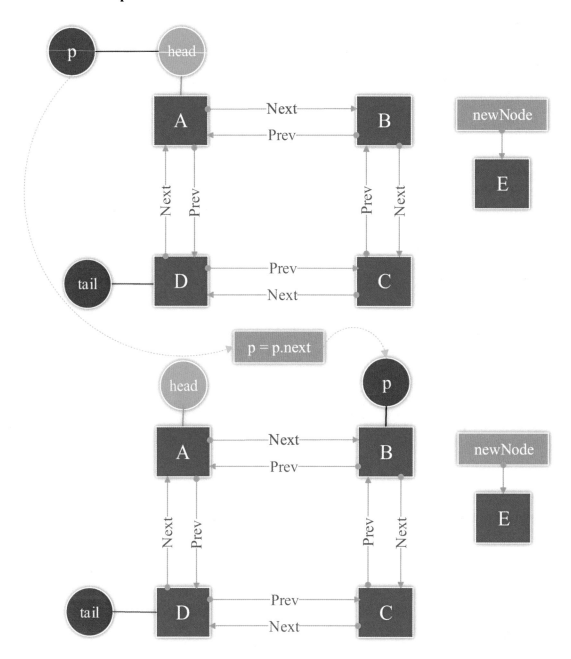

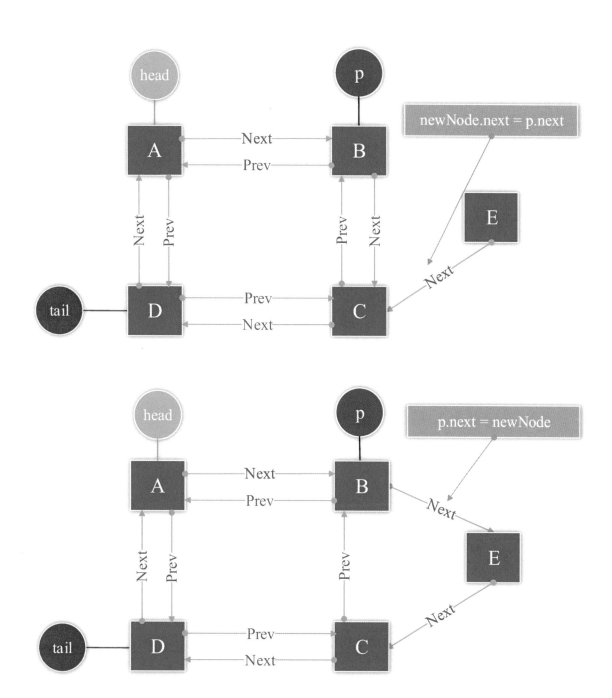

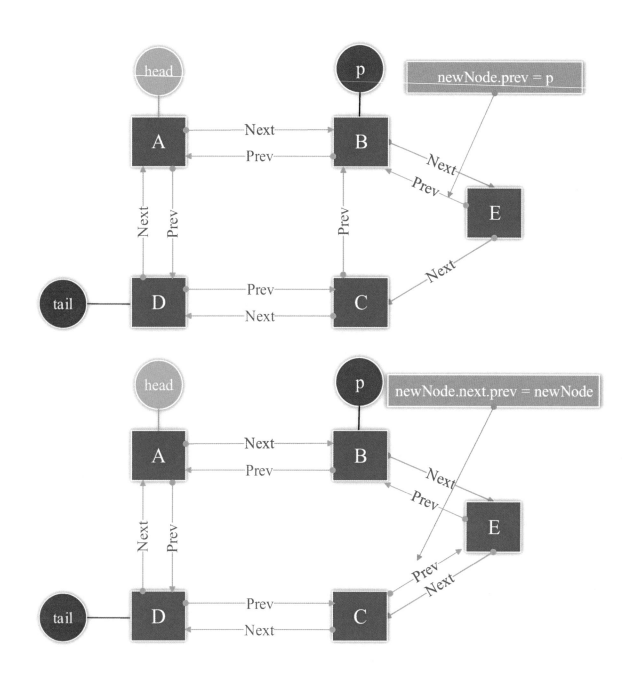

TestDoubleCircleLink.java

```java
public class TestDoubleCircleLink {
    private static Node head;
    private static Node tail;

    public static void init() {
        // the first node called head node
        head = new Node("A");
        head.next = null;
        head.prev = null;

        Node nodeB = new Node("B");
        nodeB.next = null;
        nodeB.prev = head;
        head.next = nodeB;

        Node nodeC = new Node("C");
        nodeC.next = null;
        nodeC.prev = nodeB;
        nodeB.next = nodeC;

        // the last node called tail node
        tail = new Node("D");
        tail.next = head;
        tail.prev = nodeC;
        nodeC.next = tail;
        head.prev = tail;
    }

    public static void insert(int insertPosition, Node newNode) {
        Node p = head;
        int i = 0;
        //Move the node to the insertion position
        while (p.next != null && i < insertPosition - 1) {
            p = p.next;
            i++;
        }
        newNode.next = p.next;
        p.next = newNode;
        newNode.prev = p;
        newNode.next.prev = newNode;
    }
}
```

```java
public static void print() {
    Node p = head;
    do { // From the beginning to the end
        String data = p.getData();
        System.out.print(data + " -> ");
        p = p.next;
    } while (p != head);

    String data = p.getData();
    System.out.print(data + "\n\n");

    p = tail;
    do {// From the end to beginning
        data = p.getData();
        System.out.print(data + " -> ");
        p = p.prev;
    } while (p != tail);

    data = p.getData();
    System.out.print(data + "\n\n");
}

public static void main(String[] args) {
    init();
    insert(2,new Node("E"));
    print();
}
}
```

Result:

A -> B -> E -> C -> D -> A

D -> C -> E -> B -> A -> D

4. Delete the node at index=2.

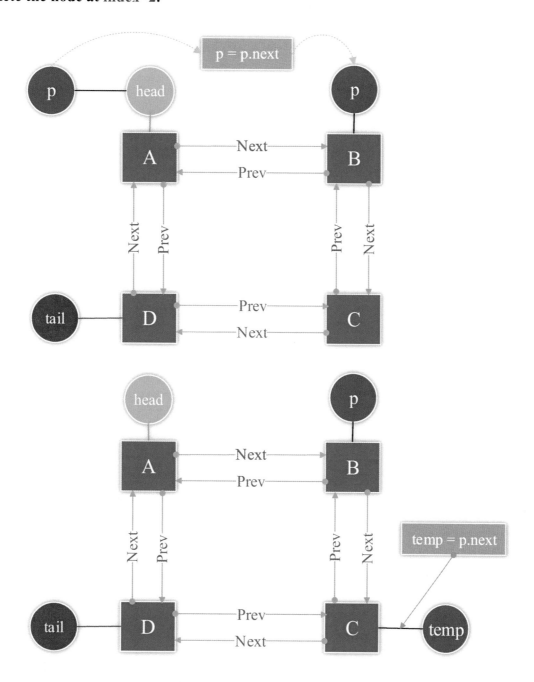

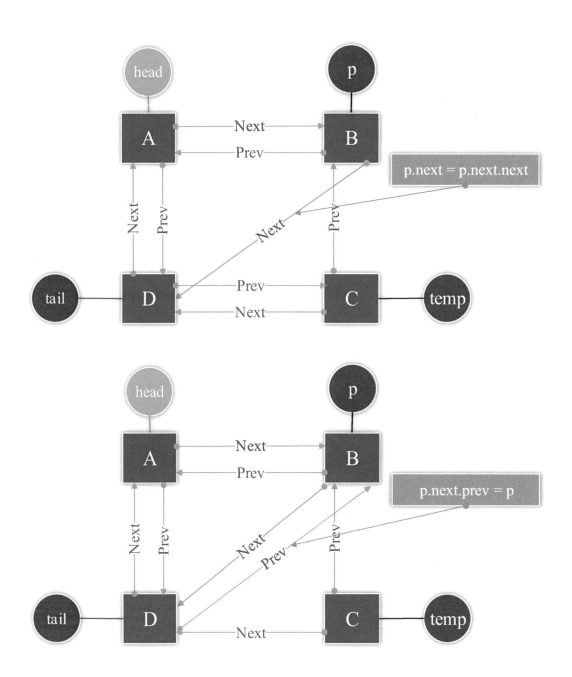

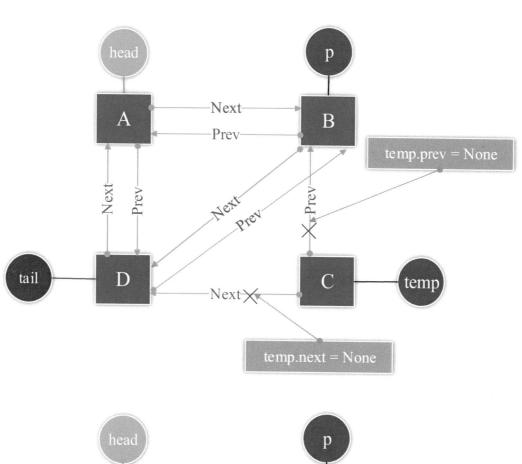

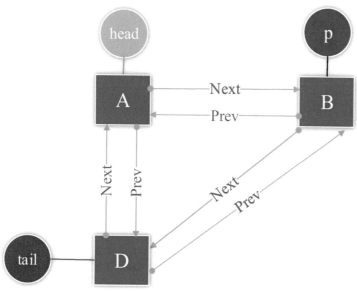

TestDoubleCircleLink.java

```java
public class TestDoubleCircleLink {
    private static Node head;
    private static Node tail;

    public static void init() {
        head = new Node("A");
        head.next = null;
        head.prev = null;

        Node nodeB = new Node("B");
        nodeB.next = null;
        nodeB.prev = head;
        head.next = nodeB;

        Node nodeC = new Node("C");
        nodeC.next = null;
        nodeC.prev = nodeB;
        nodeB.next = nodeC;

        // the last node called tail node
        tail = new Node("D");
        tail.next = head;
        tail.prev = nodeC;
        nodeC.next = tail;
        head.prev = tail;
    }

    public static void remove(int removePosition) {
        Node p = head;
        int i = 0;
        // Move the node to the previous node  that want to delete
        while (p.next != null && i < removePosition - 1) {
            p = p.next;
            i++;
        }
        Node temp = p.next;
        p.next = p.next.next;
        p.next.prev = p;
        temp.next = null;//Set the delete node next to null
        temp.prev = null;// Set the delete node prev to null
    }
```

82

```java
public static void print() {
    Node p = head;
    do {// From the beginning to the end
        String data = p.getData();
        System.out.print(data + " -> ");
        p = p.next;
    } while (p != head);

    String data = p.getData();
    System.out.print(data + "\n\n");

    p = tail;
    do {// From the end to beginning
        data = p.getData();
        System.out.print(data + " -> ");
        p = p.prev;
    } while (p != tail);

    data = p.getData();
    System.out.print(data + "\n\n");
}

public static void main(String[] args) {
    init();
    remove(2);
    print();
}
}
```

Result:

A -> B -> D -> A

D -> B -> A -> D

Queue

Queue: A Queue is a linear structure which follows a particular order in which the operations are performed. The order is First In First Out (FIFO).

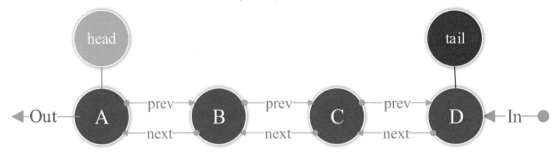

UML Diagram

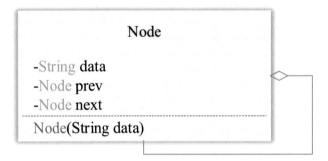

Node.java

```java
class Node {
    private String data;
    public Node next;
    public Node prev;

    public Node(String data) {
        this.data = data;
    }

    public String getData() {
        return data;
    }

    public void setData(String data) {
        this.data = data;
    }
}
```

1. Queue initialization and traversal output.

Initialization Insert A

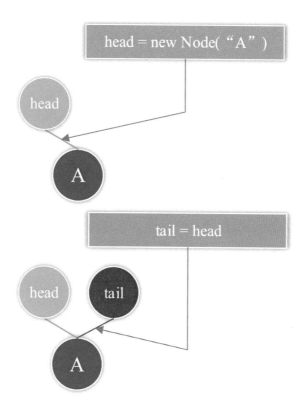

Initialization Insert B

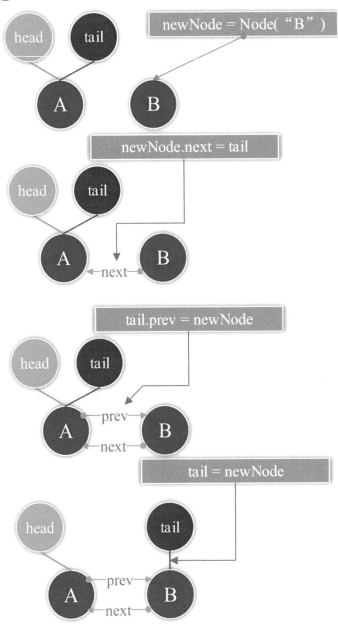

Initialization Insert C

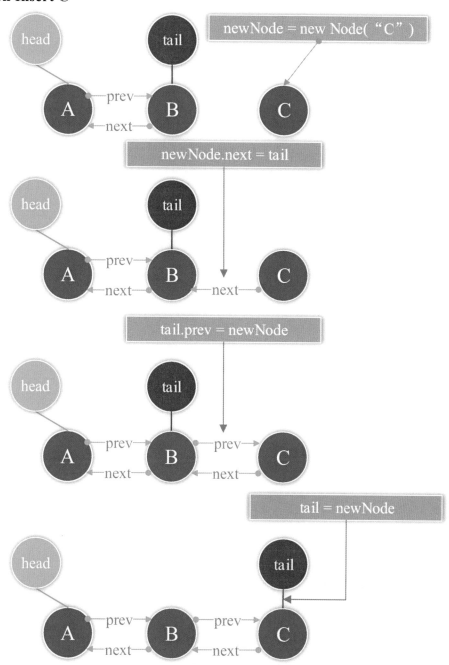

Initialization Insert D

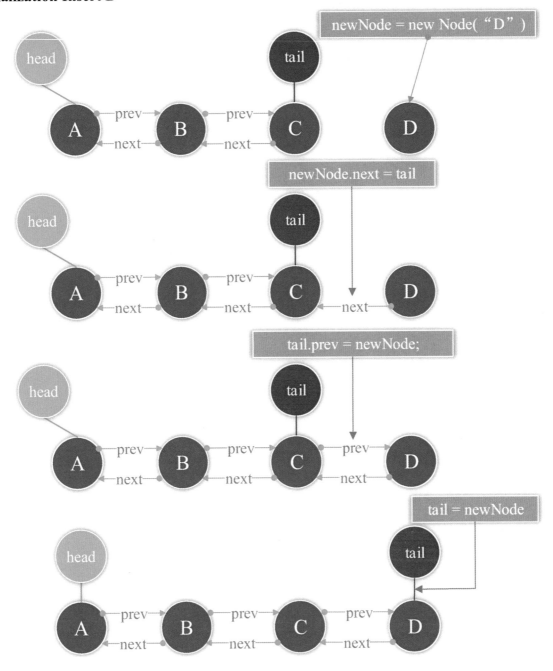

Queue.java

```java
public class Queue {

    private Node head;
    private Node tail;
    private int size; // the size of queue

    // add element to queue
    public void offer(String element) {
        if (head == null) {// if queue is empty
            head = new Node(element); // add element to head
            tail = head;
        } else {
            Node newNode = new Node(element);
            newNode.next = tail;
            tail.prev = newNode;
            tail = newNode;
        }
        size++;
    }

    // get the head and then remove head element from queue
    public Node poll() {
        Node p = head;
        if (p == null) {
            return null;
        }

        head = head.prev;
        p.next = null;
        p.prev = null;
        size--;
        return p;
    }

    public int size() {
        return size;
    }
}
```

TestQueue.java

```java
public class TestQueue {

  public static void main(String[] args) {

    Queue queue = new Queue();
    queue.offer("A");
    queue.offer("B");
    queue.offer("C");
    queue.offer("D");

    print(queue);
  }

  public static void print(Queue queue) {
    System.out.print("Head ");
    Node node = null;
    while ((node = queue.poll())!=null) {
      System.out.print(node.getData() + " <- ");
    }
    System.out.print("Tail\n");
  }

}
```

Result:
Head A <- B <- C <- D <- Tail

Stack

Stack: Stack is a linear data structure which follows a particular order in which the operations are performed. The order may be LIFO(Last In First Out).

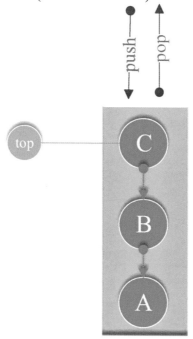

UML Diagram

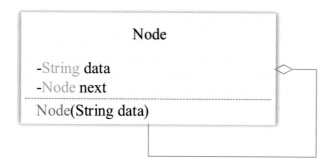

Node.java

```java
class Node {
    public String data;
    public Node next;

    public Node(String data) {
        this.data = data;
    }
}
```

1. Stack initialization and traversal output.

Push A into Stack

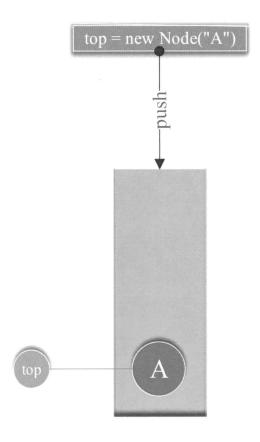

Push B into Stack

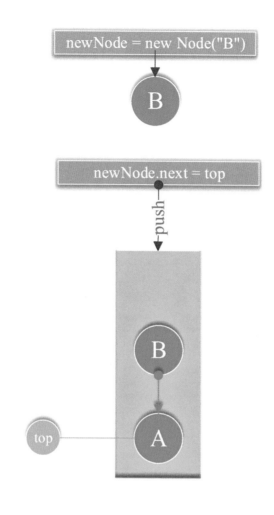

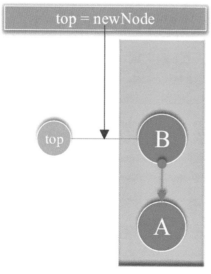

Push C into Stack

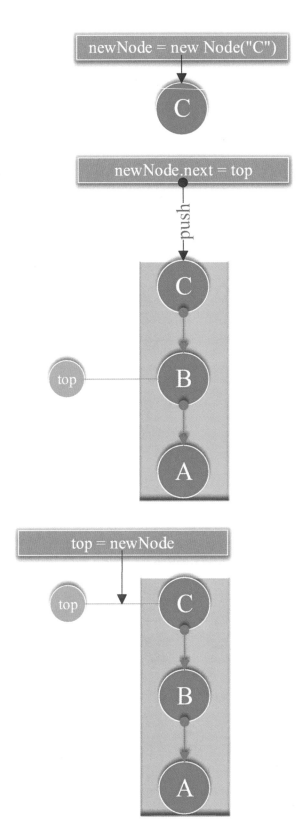

If pop C from Stack:

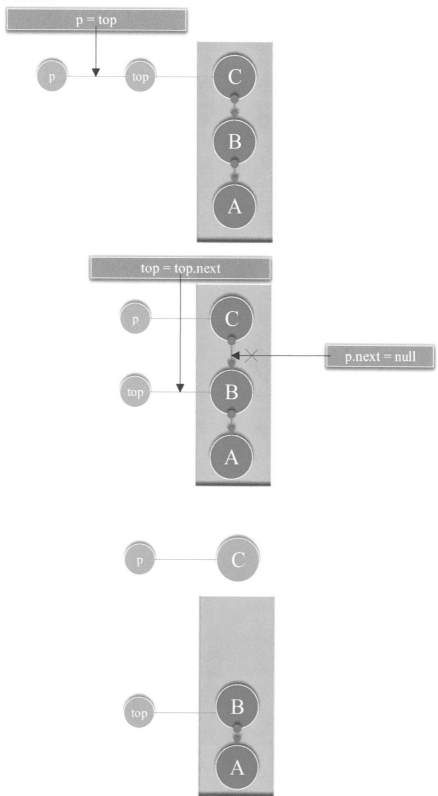

If pop B from Stack:

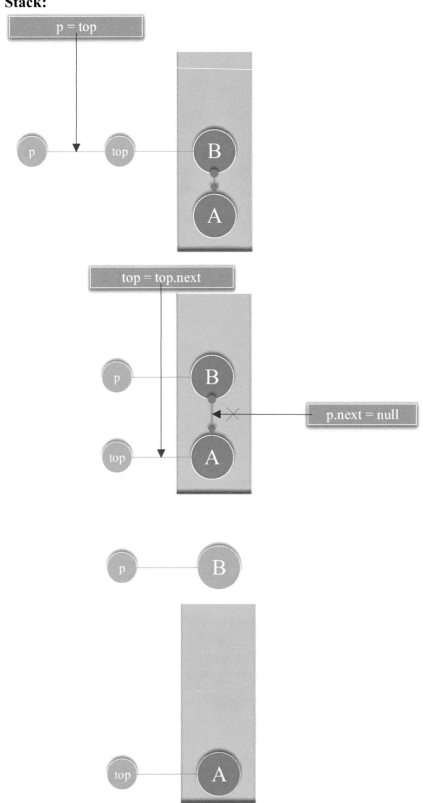

If pop A from Stack:

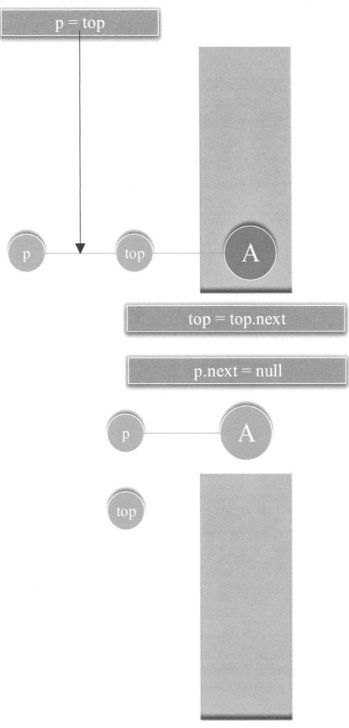

Stack.java

```java
public class Stack {

    private Node top;
    private int size; // The size of stack

    // add a element to the top of stack
    public void push(String element) {
        if (top == null) {
            top = new Node(element);
        } else {
            Node newNode = new Node(element);
            newNode.next = top;
            top = newNode;
        }
        size++;
    }

    // get a element and then remove from the top of stack
    public Node pop() {
        if(top == null)
        {
            return null;
        }

        Node p = top;
        top = top.next;// top move down

        p.next = null;
        size--;
        return p;
    }

    public int size() {
        return size;
    }
}
```

TestStack.java

```java
public class TestStack {

    public static void print(Stack stack) {
        System.out.print("Top ");
        Node node = null;
        while ((node = stack.pop())!=null) {
            System.out.print(node.data + " -> ");
        }
        System.out.print("End\n");
    }

    public static void main(String[] args) {
        Stack stack = new Stack();
        stack.push("A");
        stack.push("B");
        stack.push("C");

        print(stack);
    }

}
```

Result:

Top C -> B -> A -> End

Recursive Algorithm

Recursive Algorithm:
The program function itself calls its own to progress until it reaches a certain condition and step by step returns to the end.

1. Factorial of n : n*(n-1)*(n-2) *2*1

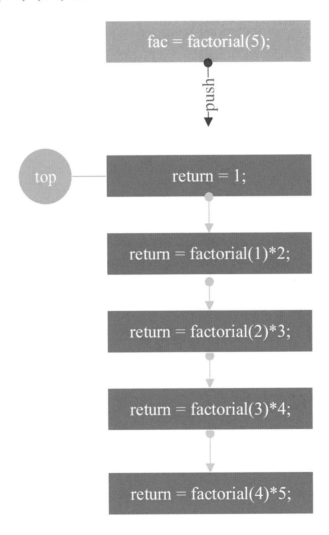

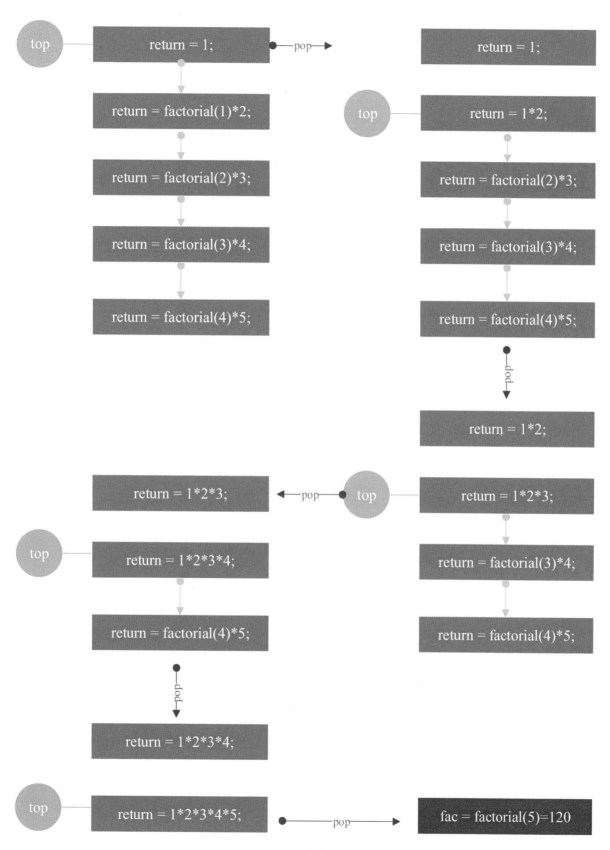

TestFactorial.java

```java
public class TestFactorial {

   public static long factorial(int n) {
      if (n == 1) {
         return 1;
      } else {
         return factorial(n - 1) * n;//Recursively call self until the end of the return
      }
   }

   public static void main(String[] args) {
      int n = 5;
      long fac = factorial(n);
      System.out.println("The factorial of 5 is :" + fac);
   }
}
```

Result:

The factorial of 5 is :120

Quick Sort Algorithm

Quick Sort Algorithm:
Quicksort is a popular sorting algorithm that is often faster in practice compared to other sorting algorithms. It utilizes a divide-and-conquer strategy to quickly sort data items by dividing a large array into two smaller arrays.

1. The scores {90, 60, 50, 80, 70, 100} by quick sort

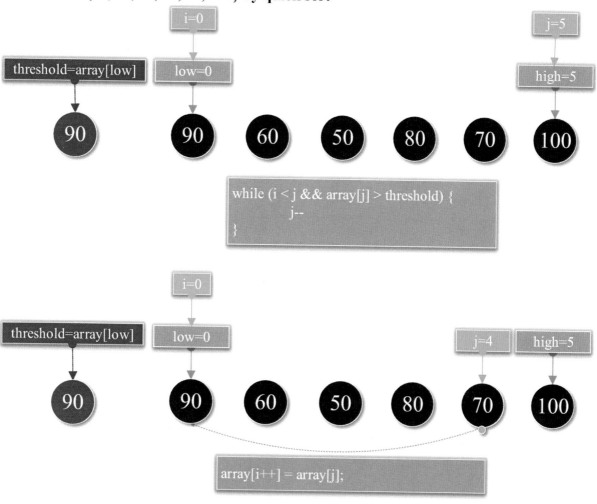

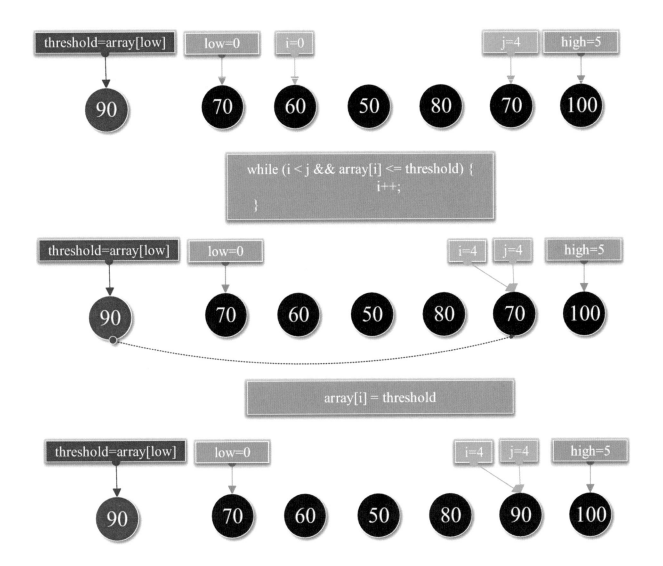

threshold=array[low] low=0 i=0 j=4 high=5

90 70 60 50 80 70 100

while (i < j && array[i] <= threshold) {
i++;
}

threshold=array[low] low=0 i=4 j=4 high=5

90 70 60 50 80 70 100

array[i] = threshold

threshold=array[low] low=0 i=4 j=4 high=5

90 70 60 50 80 90 100

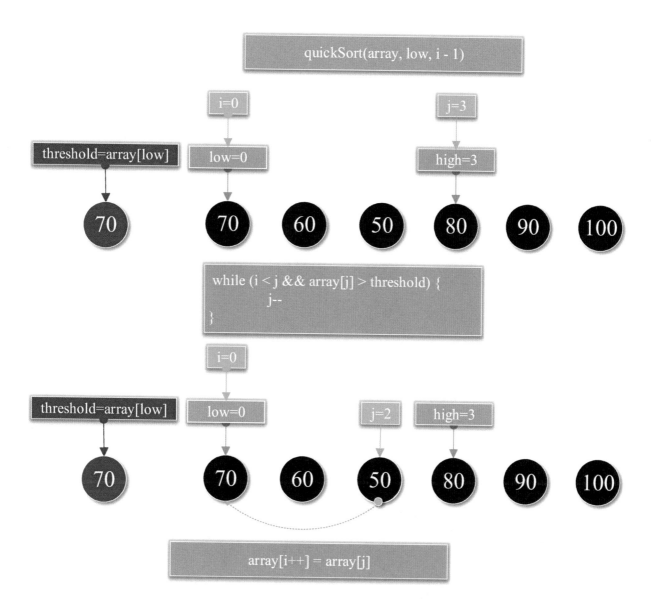

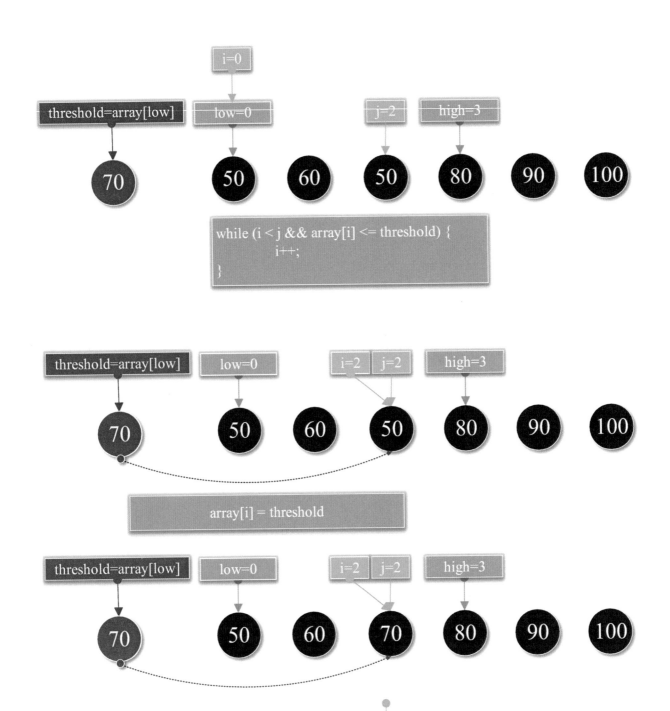

```
while (i < j && array[i] <= threshold) {
    i++;
}
```

array[i] = threshold

TestQuickSort.java

```java
public class TestQuickSort {

    private static void quickSort(int[] array, int low, int high) {
        if (low > high) {
            return;
        }
        int i = low;
        int j = high;
        int threshold = array[low];

        // Alternately scanned from both ends of the list
        while (i < j) {
            // Find the first position less than threshold from right to left
            while (i < j && array[j] > threshold) {
                j--;
            }
            //Replace the low with a smaller number than the threshold
            if (i < j)
                array[i++] = array[j];

            // Find the first position greater than threshold from left to right
            while (i < j && array[i] <= threshold) {
                i++;
            }

            //Replace the high with a number larger than the threshold
            if (i < j)
                array[j--] = array[i];
        }

        array[i] = threshold;

        quickSort(array, low, i - 1); // Recursive quickSort on the left
        quickSort(array, i + 1, high); // Recursive quickSort on the right
    }

    public static void quickSort(int[] array) {
        if (array.length > 0) {
            quickSort(array, 0, array.length - 1);
        }
    }
}
```

```java
public static void main(String[] args) {
    int[] scores = { 90, 60, 50, 80, 70, 100 };

    quickSort(scores);

    for (int i = 0; i < scores.length; i++) {
        System.out.print(scores[i] + ",");
    }
}
}
```

Result:
50,60,70,80,90,100

Big O Notation of Quick Sorting:
1. Worst and Average Case Time Complexity: O(n*n). Worst case occurs when array is reverse sorted.
2. Best Case Time Complexity: O(n*log2n). Best case occurs when array is already sorted
3. Auxiliary Space: O(log2n) - O(n)

Two-way Merge Algorithm

Two-way Merge Algorithm:
The data of the first half and the second half are sorted, and the two ordered sub-list are merged into one ordered list, which continue to recursive to the end.

1. The scores {50, 65, 99, 87, 74, 63, 76, 100} by merge sort

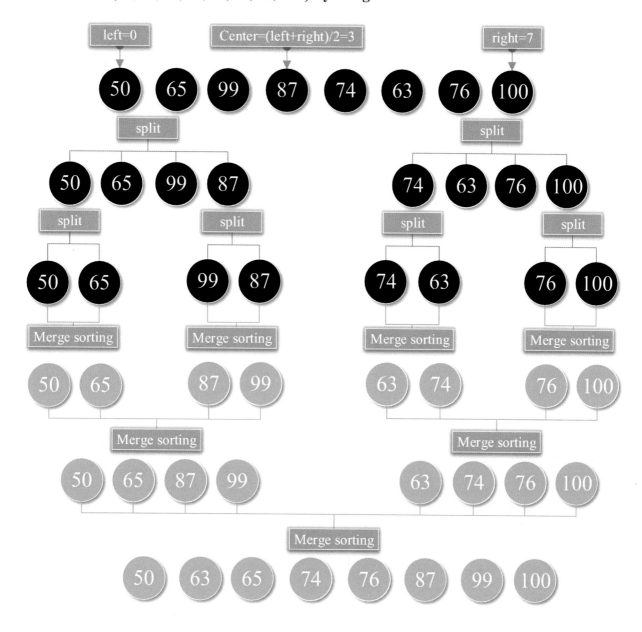

TestMergeSort.java

```java
public class TestMergeSort {

  private static void mergeSort(int[] array) {
    mergeSort(array, new int[array.length], 0, array.length - 1);
  }

  private static void mergeSort(int[] array, int[] temp, int left, int right) {
    if (left < right) {
      int center = (left + right) / 2;
      mergeSort(array, temp, left, center); // Recursive mergeSort on the left
      mergeSort(array, temp, center + 1, right); // Recursive mergeSort on the right
      merge(array, temp, left, center + 1, right); // Merge two ordered arrays
    }
  }

  private static void merge(int[] array, int[] temp, int left, int right, int rightEndIndex) {
    int leftEndIndex = right - 1; // End subscript on the left
    int tempIndex = left; // Starting from the left
    int elementNumber = rightEndIndex - left + 1;
    // Merge two ordered arrays
    while (left <= leftEndIndex && right <= rightEndIndex) {
      if (array[left] <= array[right])
        temp[tempIndex++] = array[left++];
      else
        temp[tempIndex++] = array[right++];
    }

    while (left <= leftEndIndex) { // If there is element on the left
      temp[tempIndex++] = array[left++];
    }

    while (right <= rightEndIndex) { // If there is element on the right
      temp[tempIndex++] = array[right++];
    }

    // Copy temp to array
    for (int i = 0; i < elementNumber; i++) {
      array[rightEndIndex] = temp[rightEndIndex];
      rightEndIndex--;
    }
  }
}
```

```
    public static void main(String args[]) {
      int scores[] = { 50, 65, 99, 87, 74, 63, 76, 100, 92 };

      mergeSort(scores);

      for (int i = 0; i < scores.length; i++) {
        System.out.print(scores[i] + ",");
      }
    }
}
```

Result:
50,63,65,74,76,87,99,100

Big O Notation of Merge Sorting:
1. Worst and Average Case Time Complexity: $O(n*log2n)$. Worst case occurs when array is reverse sorted.
2. Best Case Time Complexity: $O(n*log2n)$. Best case occurs when array is already sorted
3. Auxiliary Space: $O(n)$

Binary Search Tree

Binary Search Tree:
1. If the left subtree of any node is not empty, the value of all nodes on the left subtree is less than the value of its root node;
2. If the right subtree of any node is not empty, the value of all nodes on the right subtree is greater than the value of its root node;
3. The left subtree and the right subtree of any node are also binary search trees.

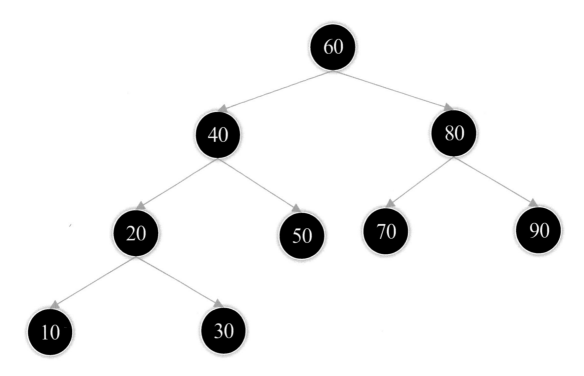

Node UML Diagram

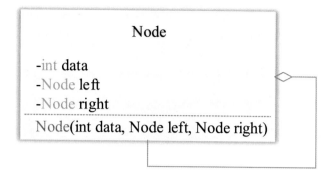

Node.java

```java
public class Node {

    private int data;
    public Node left;
    public Node right;

    public Node() {
    }

    public Node(int data, Node left, Node right) {
        this.data = data;
        this.left = left;
        this.right = right;
    }

    public int getData() {
        return data;
    }

    public void setData(int data) {
        this.data = data;
    }

}
```

1.Construct a binary search tree, insert node

The inserted nodes are compared from the root node, and the smaller than the root node is compared with the left subtree of the root node, otherwise, compared with the right subtree until the left subtree is empty or the right subtree is empty, then is inserted.

Insert 60

Insert 40

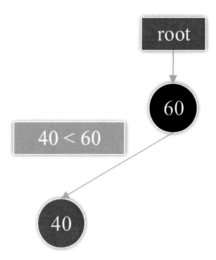

Insert 20

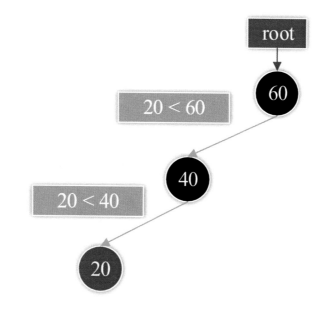

Insert 10

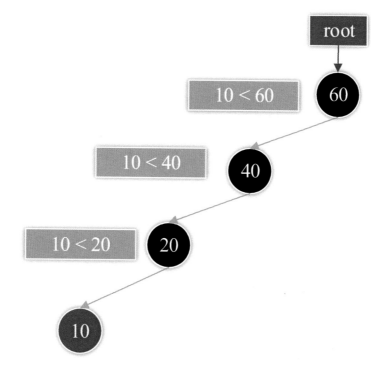

Insert 30

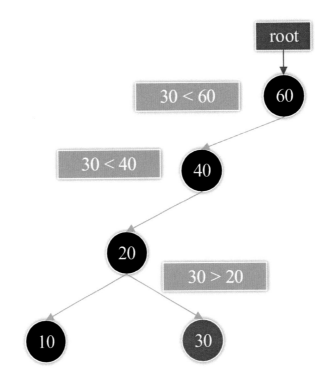

Insert 50

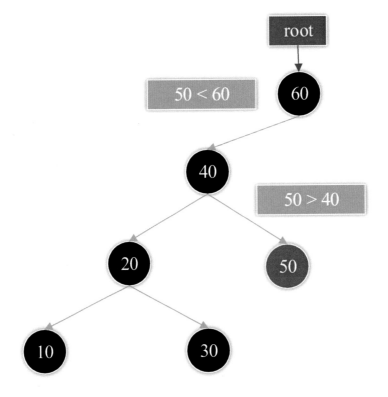

Insert 80

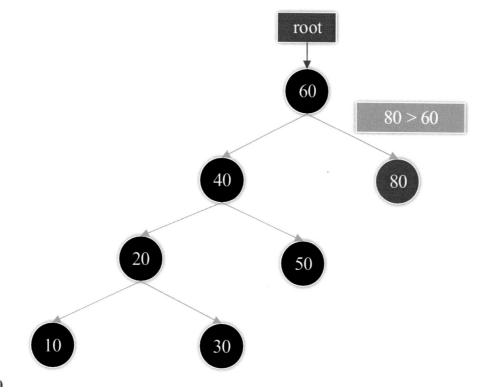

Insert 70

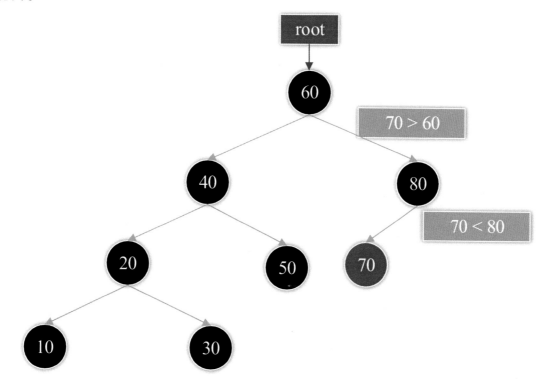

Insert 90

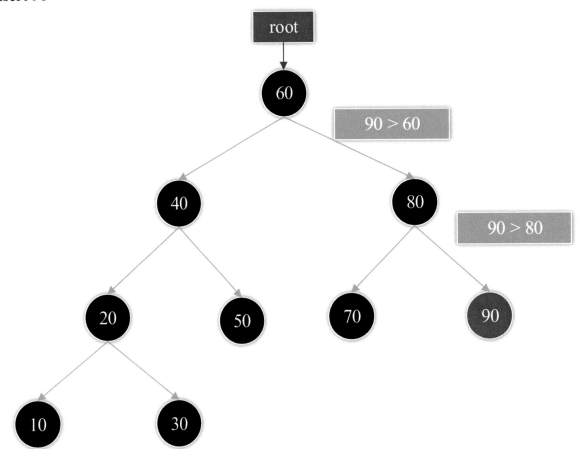

2. binary search tree In-order traversal
In-order traversal : left subtree -> root node -> right subtree

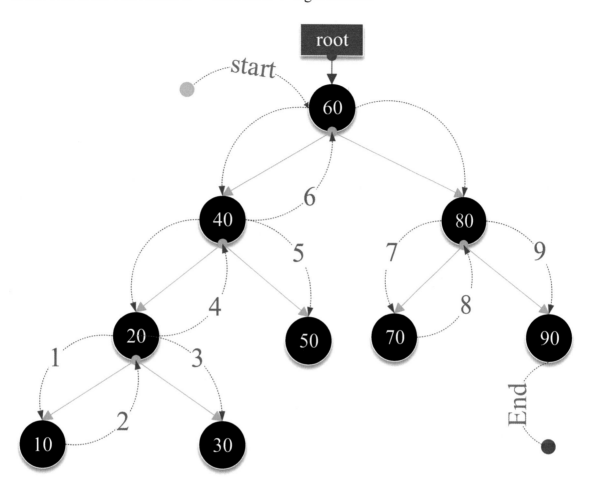

Result:

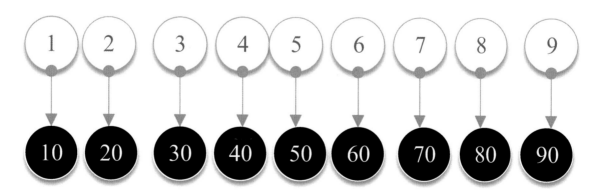

BinaryTree.java

```java
public class BinaryTree {
    private Node root;

    public Node getRoot() {
        return root;
    }

    public void inOrder(Node root) {
        if (root == null) {
            return;
        }
        inOrder(root.left); // Traversing the left subtree
        System.out.print(root.getData() + ", ");
        inOrder(root.right); // Traversing the right subtree
    }

    public void insert(Node node, int newData) {
        if (this.root == null) {
            this.root = new Node(newData, null, null);
            return;
        }

        int compareValue = newData - node.getData();
        //Recursive left subtree, continue to find the insertion position
        if (compareValue < 0) {
            if (node.left == null) {
                node.left = new Node(newData, null, null);
            } else {
                insert(node.left, newData);
            }
        } else if (compareValue > 0) {//Recursive right subtree to find the insertion position
            if (node.right == null) {
                node.right = new Node(newData, null, null);
            } else {
                insert(node.right, newData);
            }
        }
    }
}
```

TestBinaryTree.java

```java
public class TestBinaryTree {

    public static void main(String[] args) {
        BinaryTree binaryTree=new BinaryTree();

        //Constructing a binary search tree
        binaryTree.insert(binaryTree.getRoot(), 60);
        binaryTree.insert(binaryTree.getRoot(), 40);
        binaryTree.insert(binaryTree.getRoot(), 20);
        binaryTree.insert(binaryTree.getRoot(), 10);
        binaryTree.insert(binaryTree.getRoot(), 30);
        binaryTree.insert(binaryTree.getRoot(), 50);
        binaryTree.insert(binaryTree.getRoot(), 80);
        binaryTree.insert(binaryTree.getRoot(), 70);
        binaryTree.insert(binaryTree.getRoot(), 90);

        System.out.println("\nIn-order traversal binary search tree");
        binaryTree.inOrder(binaryTree.getRoot());
    }

}
```

Result:
In-order traversal binary search tree
10, 20, 30, 40, 50, 60, 70, 80, 90,

3. binary search tree Pre-order traversal
Pre-order traversal : root node -> left subtree -> right subtree

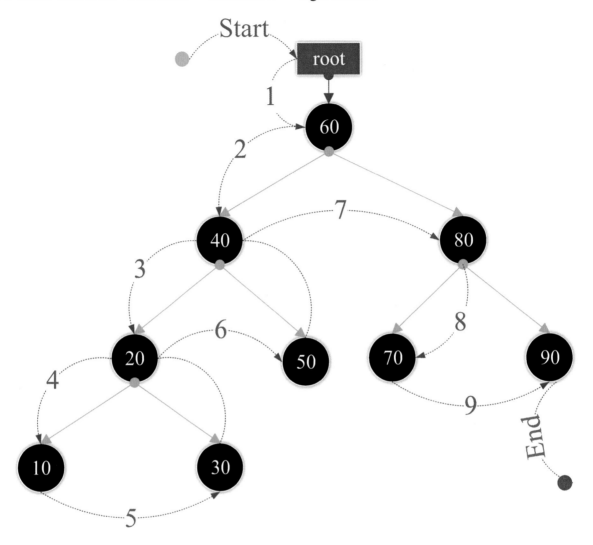

Result:

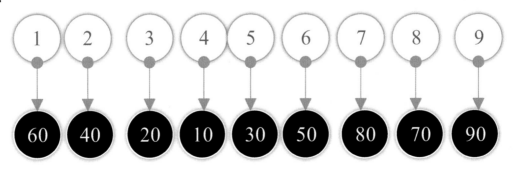

BinaryTree.java

```java
public class BinaryTree {
   private Node root;

   public Node getRoot() {
      return root;
   }

   public void preOrder(Node  root) {
      if (root == null) {
         return;
      }
      System.out.print(root.getData() + ", ");
      preOrder(root.left); // Recursive Traversing the left subtree
      preOrder(root.right); // Recursive Traversing the right subtree
   }

   public void insert(Node node, int newData) {
      if (this.root == null) {
         this.root = new Node(newData, null, null);
         return;
      }

      int compareValue = newData - node.getData();
      //Recursive left subtree, continue to find the insertion position
      if (compareValue < 0) {
         if (node.left == null) {
            node.left = new Node(newData, null, null);
         } else {
            insert(node.left, newData);
         }
      } else if (compareValue > 0) {//Recursive right subtree to find the insertion position
         if (node.right == null) {
            node.right = new Node(newData, null, null);
         } else {
            insert(node.right, newData);
         }
      }
   }
}
```

TestBinaryTree.java

```java
public class TestBinaryTree {

    public static void main(String[] args) {
        BinaryTree binaryTree=new BinaryTree();

        //Constructing a binary search tree
        binaryTree.insert(binaryTree.getRoot(), 60);
        binaryTree.insert(binaryTree.getRoot(), 40);
        binaryTree.insert(binaryTree.getRoot(), 20);
        binaryTree.insert(binaryTree.getRoot(), 10);
        binaryTree.insert(binaryTree.getRoot(), 30);
        binaryTree.insert(binaryTree.getRoot(), 50);
        binaryTree.insert(binaryTree.getRoot(), 80);
        binaryTree.insert(binaryTree.getRoot(), 70);
        binaryTree.insert(binaryTree.getRoot(), 90);

        System.out.println("Pre-order traversal binary search tree");
        binaryTree.preOrder(binaryTree.getRoot());
    }

}
```

Result:
Pre-order traversal binary search tree
60, 40, 20, 10, 30, 50, 80, 70, 90,

4. binary search tree Post-order traversal

Post-order traversal : right subtree -> root node -> left subtree

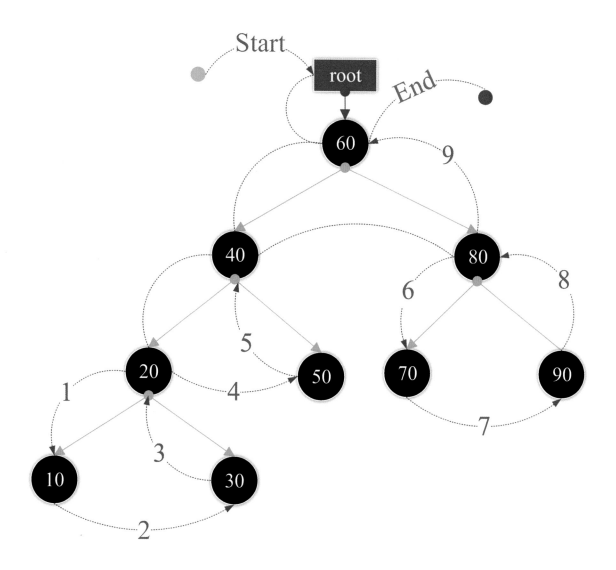

Result:

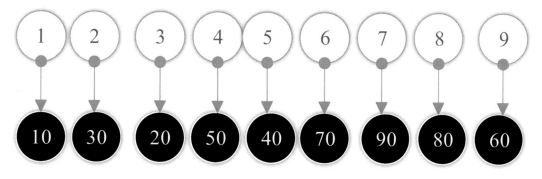

BinaryTree.java

```java
public class BinaryTree {
    private Node root;

    public Node getRoot() {
        return root;
    }

    public void postOrder(Node root) {
        if (root == null) {
            return;
        }
        postOrder(root.left); // Recursive Traversing the left subtree
        postOrder(root.right); // Recursive Traversing the right subtree
        System.out.print(root.getData() + ", ");
    }

    public void insert(Node node, int newData) {
        if (this.root == null) {
            this.root = new Node(newData, null, null);
            return;
        }
        int compareValue = newData - node.getData();

        //Recursive left subtree, continue to find the insertion position
        if (compareValue < 0) {
            if (node.left == null) {
                node.left = new Node(newData, null, null);
            } else {
                insert(node.left, newData);
            }
        } else if (compareValue > 0) {//Recursive right subtree to find the insertion position
            if (node.right == null) {
                node.right = new Node(newData, null, null);
            } else {
                insert(node.right, newData);
            }
        }
    }
}
```

TestBinaryTree.java

```java
public class TestBinaryTree {

    public static void main(String[] args) {
        BinaryTree binaryTree=new BinaryTree();

        //Constructing a binary search tree
        binaryTree.insert(binaryTree.getRoot(), 60);
        binaryTree.insert(binaryTree.getRoot(), 40);
        binaryTree.insert(binaryTree.getRoot(), 20);
        binaryTree.insert(binaryTree.getRoot(), 10);
        binaryTree.insert(binaryTree.getRoot(), 30);
        binaryTree.insert(binaryTree.getRoot(), 50);
        binaryTree.insert(binaryTree.getRoot(), 80);
        binaryTree.insert(binaryTree.getRoot(), 70);
        binaryTree.insert(binaryTree.getRoot(), 90);

        System.out.println("Post-order traversal binary search tree");
        binaryTree.postOrder(binaryTree.getRoot());
    }
}
```

Result:
Post-order traversal binary search tree
10, 30, 20, 50, 40, 70, 90, 80, 60,

5. binary search tree Maximum and minimum

Minimum value: The small value is on the left child node, as long as the recursion traverses the left child until be empty, the current node is the minimum node.

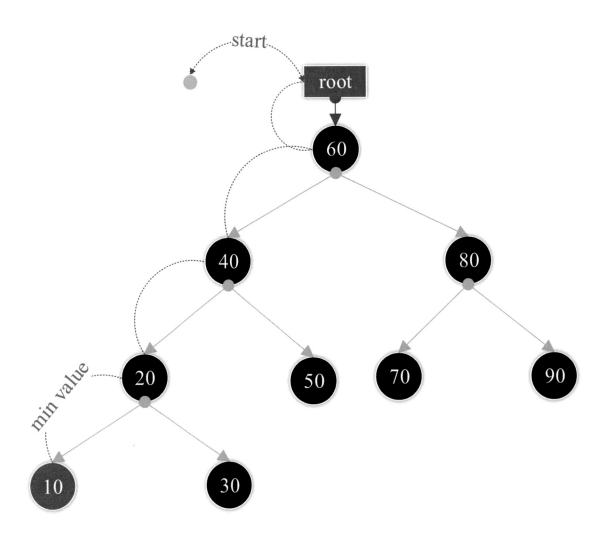

Maximum value: The large value is on the right child node, as long as the recursive traversal is the right child until be empty, the current node is the largest node.

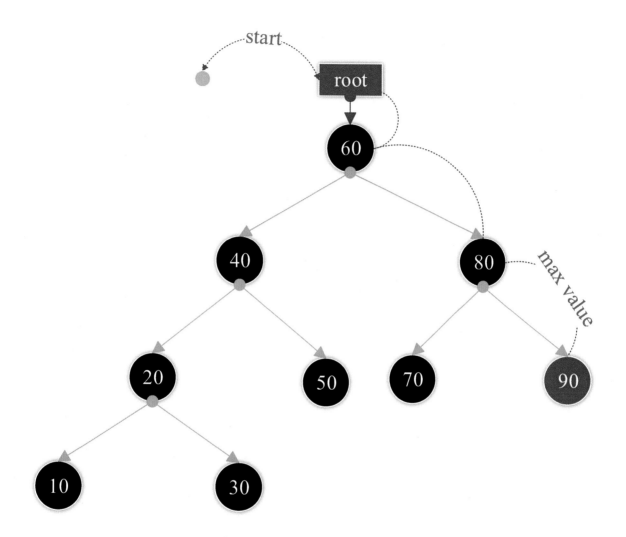

BinaryTree.java

```java
public class BinaryTree {
  private Node root;

  public Node getRoot() {
    return root;
  }

  //Minimum value
  public Node searchMinValue(Node node) {
    if (node == null || node.getData() == 0)
      return null;
    if (node.left == null) {
      return node;
    }
    //Recursively find the minimum from the left subtree
    return searchMinValue(node.left);
  }

  //Maximum value
  public Node searchMaxValue(Node node) {
    if (node == null || node.getData() == 0)
      return null;
    if (node.right == null) {
      return node;
    }
    //Recursively find the minimum from the right subtree
    return searchMaxValue(node.right);
  }
}
```

```java
public void insert(Node node, int newData) {
    if (this.root == null) {
        this.root = new Node(newData, null, null);
        return;
    }

    int compareValue = newData - node.getData();

    //Recursive left subtree, continue to find the insertion position
    if (compareValue < 0) {
        if (node.left == null) {
            node.left = new Node(newData, null, null);
        } else {
            insert(node.left, newData);
        }
    } else if (compareValue > 0) {//Recursive right subtree to find the insertion position
        if (node.right == null) {
            node.right = new Node(newData, null, null);
        } else {
            insert(node.right, newData);
        }
    }
}
```

TestBinaryTree.java

```java
public class TestBinaryTree {

    public static void main(String[] args) {
        BinaryTree binaryTree=new BinaryTree();

        //Constructing a binary search tree
        binaryTree.insert(binaryTree.getRoot(), 60);
        binaryTree.insert(binaryTree.getRoot(), 40);
        binaryTree.insert(binaryTree.getRoot(), 20);
        binaryTree.insert(binaryTree.getRoot(), 10);
        binaryTree.insert(binaryTree.getRoot(), 30);
        binaryTree.insert(binaryTree.getRoot(), 50);
        binaryTree.insert(binaryTree.getRoot(), 80);
        binaryTree.insert(binaryTree.getRoot(), 70);
        binaryTree.insert(binaryTree.getRoot(), 90);

        System.out.println("\nMinimum Value");
        Node minNode=binaryTree.searchMinValue(binaryTree.getRoot());
        System.out.println(minNode.getData());

        System.out.println("\nMaximum Value");
        Node maxNode=binaryTree.searchMaxValue(binaryTree.getRoot());
        System.out.println(maxNode.getData());
    }
}
```

Result:
Minimum Value
10

Maximum Value
90

6. binary search tree Delete Node

Binary search tree delete node 3 cases
1. If there is no child node, delete it directly
2. If there is only one child node, the child node replaces the current node, and then deletes the current node.
3. If there are two child nodes, replace the current node with the smallest node from the right subtree, because the smallest node on the right is also larger than the value on the left.

1. If there is no child node, delete it directly: delete node 10

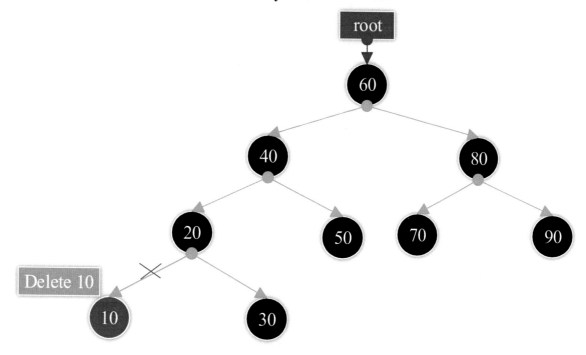

2. If there is only one child node, the child node replaces the current node, and then deletes the current node. Delete node 20

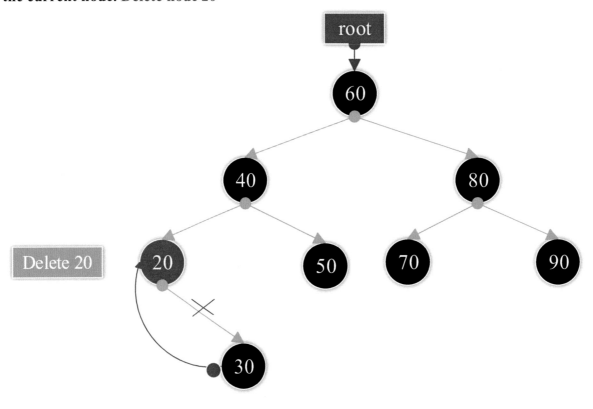

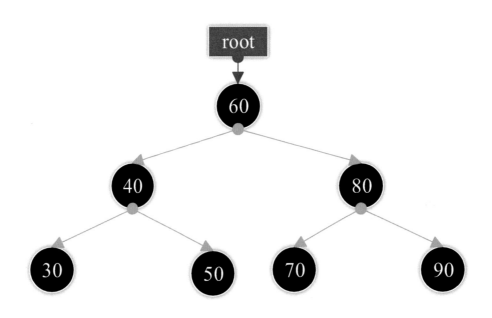

3. If there are two child nodes, replace the current node with the smallest node from the right subtree, Delete node 40

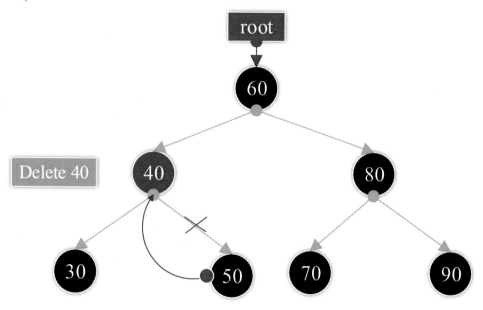

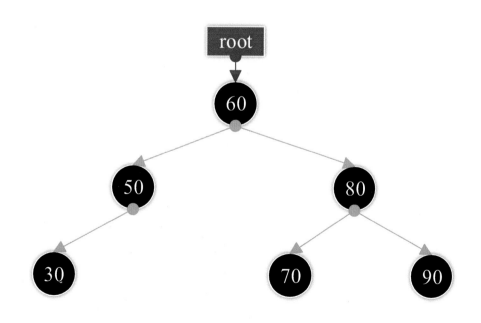

BinaryTree.java

```java
public class BinaryTree {
  private Node root;

  public Node getRoot() {
    return root;
  }

  public void inOrder(Node root) {
    if (root == null) {
      return;
    }
    inOrder(root.left); // Traversing the left subtree
    System.out.print(root.getData() + ", ");
    inOrder(root.right); // Traversing the right subtree
  }

  public Node remove(Node node, int newData) {
    if (node == null)
      return node;
    int compareValue = newData - node.getData();
    if (compareValue > 0) {
      node.right = remove(node.right, newData);
    } else if (compareValue < 0) {
      node.left = remove(node.left, newData);
    } else if (node.left != null && node.right != null) {
      //Find the minimum node of the right subtree to replace the current node
      node.setData(searchMinValue(node.right).getData());
      node.right = remove(node.right, node.getData());
    } else {
      node = (node.left != null) ? node.left : node.right;
    }
    return node;

  }
```

```java
//Search minimum
public Node searchMinValue(Node node) {
    if (node == null || node.getData() == 0)
        return null;
    if (node.left == null) {
        return node;
    }
    return searchMinValue(node.left);//Recursively find the minimum from the left subtree
}

public void insert(Node node, int newData) {
    if (this.root == null) {
        this.root = new Node(newData, null, null);
        return;
    }

    int compareValue = newData - node.getData();

    //Recursive left subtree, continue to find the insertion position
    if (compareValue < 0) {
        if (node.left == null) {
            node.left = new Node(newData, null, null);
        } else {
            insert(node.left, newData);
        }
    } else if (compareValue > 0) {//Recursive right subtree to find the insertion position
        if (node.right == null) {
            node.right = new Node(newData, null, null);
        } else {
            insert(node.right, newData);
        }
    }
}
```

TestBinaryTree.java

```java
public class TestBinaryTree {

  public static void main(String[] args) {
    BinaryTree binaryTree=new BinaryTree();
    //Constructing a binary search tree
    binaryTree.insert(binaryTree.getRoot(), 60);
    binaryTree.insert(binaryTree.getRoot(), 40);
    binaryTree.insert(binaryTree.getRoot(), 20);
    binaryTree.insert(binaryTree.getRoot(), 10);
    binaryTree.insert(binaryTree.getRoot(), 30);
    binaryTree.insert(binaryTree.getRoot(), 50);
    binaryTree.insert(binaryTree.getRoot(), 80);
    binaryTree.insert(binaryTree.getRoot(), 70);
    binaryTree.insert(binaryTree.getRoot(), 90);

    System.out.println("\ndelete node is:  10");
    binaryTree.remove(binaryTree.getRoot(), 10);

    System.out.println("\nIn-order traversal binary tree");
    binaryTree.inOrder(binaryTree.getRoot());

    System.out.println("\n-----------------------------------------");

    System.out.println("\ndelete node is:  20");
    binaryTree.remove(binaryTree.getRoot(), 20);

    System.out.println("\nIn-order traversal binary tree");
    binaryTree.inOrder(binaryTree.getRoot());

    System.out.println("\n-----------------------------------------");

    System.out.println("\ndelete node is:  40");
    binaryTree.remove(binaryTree.getRoot(), 40);

    System.out.println("\nIn-order traversal binary tree");
    binaryTree.inOrder(binaryTree.getRoot());
  }
}
```

Result:

delete node is: 10

In-order traversal binary tree
20 , 30 , 40 , 50 , 60 , 70 , 80 , 90 ,
----

delete node is: 20

In-order traversal binary tree
30 , 40 , 50 , 60 , 70 , 80 , 90 ,
----

delete node is: 40

In-order traversal binary tree
30 , 50 , 60 , 70 , 80 , 90 ,

Binary Heap Sorting

Binary Heap Sorting:
The value of the non-terminal node in the binary tree is not greater than the value of its left and right child nodes.

Small top heap : ki <= k2i and ki <= k2i+1
Big top heap :ki >= k2i and ki >= k2i+1

Parent node subscript = (i-1)/2
Left subnode subscript = 2*i+1
Right subnode subscript = 2*i+2

Heap sorting process:
1. Build a heap
2. After outputting the top element of the heap, adjust from top to bottom, compare the top element with the root node of its left and right subtrees, and swap the smallest element to the top of the heap; then adjust continuously until the leaf nodes to get new heap.

1. {10, 90, 20, 80, 30, 70, 40, 60, 50} build heap and then heap sort output.

Initialize the heap and build the heap

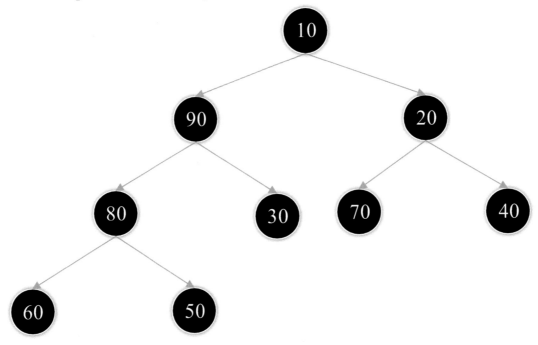

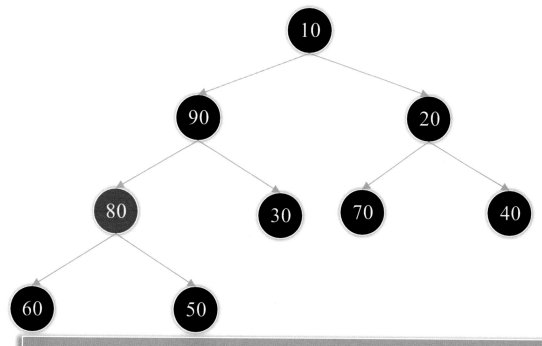

Not Leaf Node = 80 > left = 60 , 80 > right = 50 No need to move

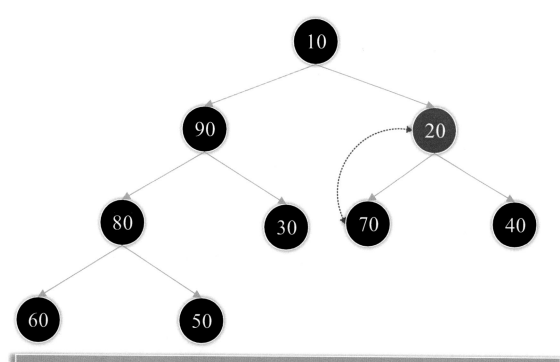

Not Leaf Node = 20 < left = 70 , 70 > right = 40 , 20 swap with 70

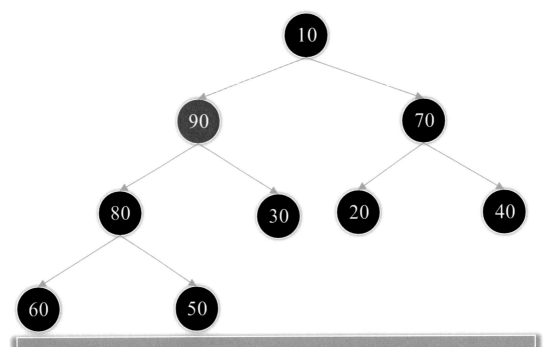

Not Leaf Node = 90 > left = 80 ,   80 > right = 30 No need to move

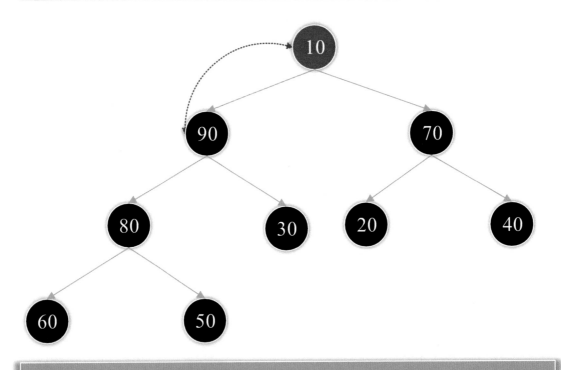

Not Leaf Node = 10 < left = 90 , 90 > right = 70   , 10 swap with 90

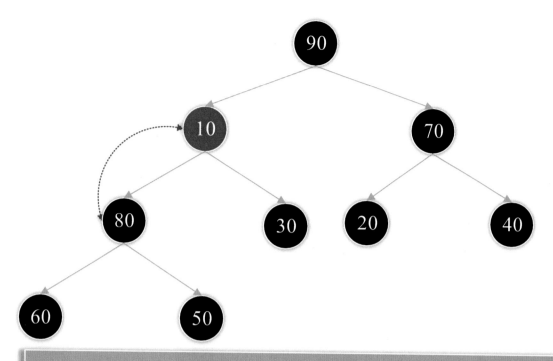

Still Not Leaf Node = 10 < left = 80 , 80 > right =30 , 10 swap with 80

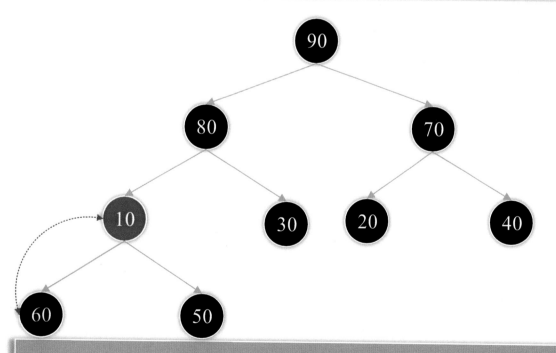

Still Not Leaf Node = 10 < left = 60 , 60 > right =50 , 10 swap with 60

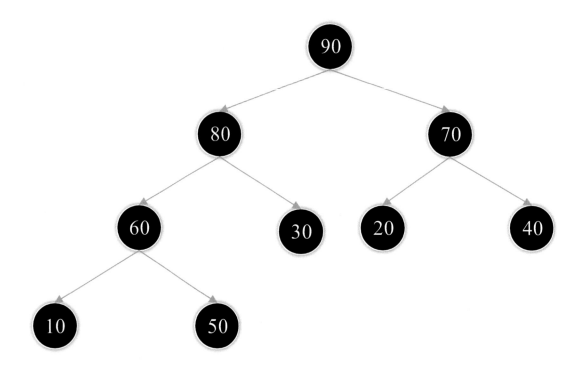

Create the heap finished

2. Start heap sorting

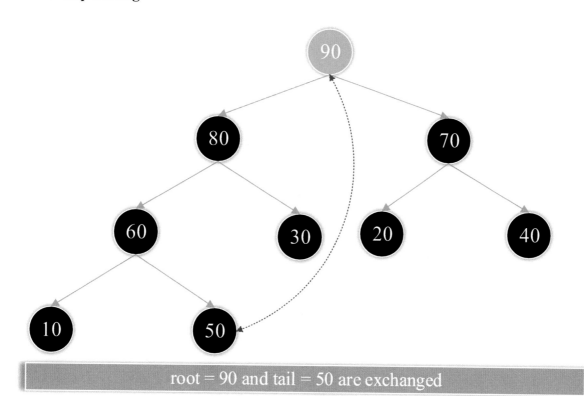

root = 90 and tail = 50 are exchanged

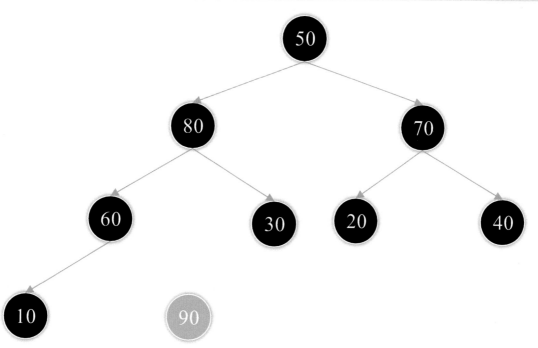

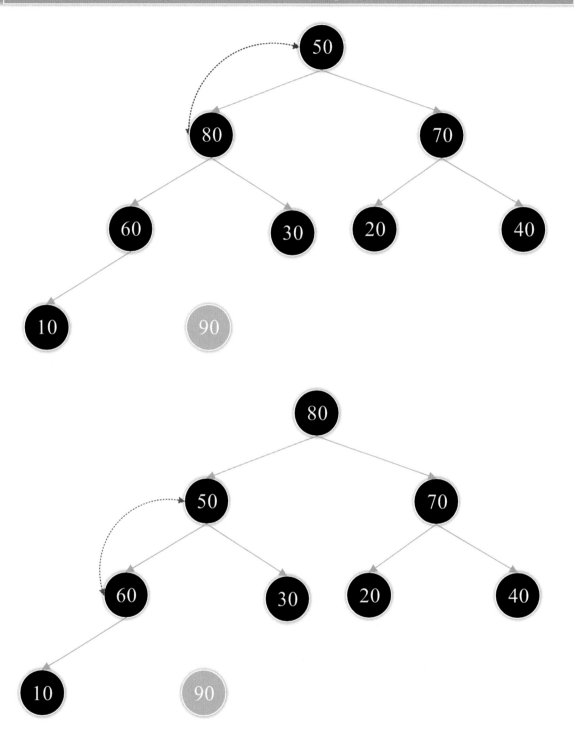

146

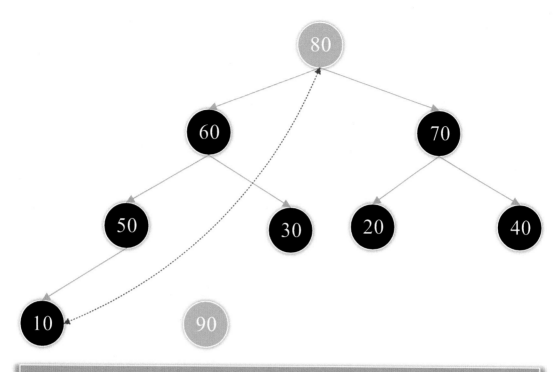

root = 80 and tail = 10 are exchanged

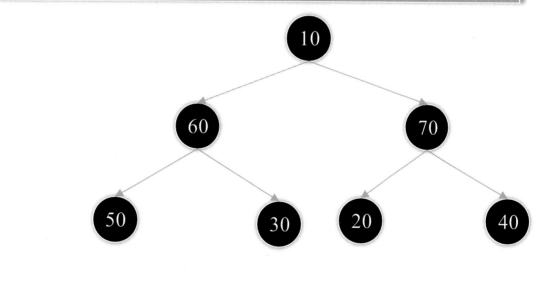

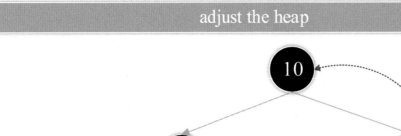

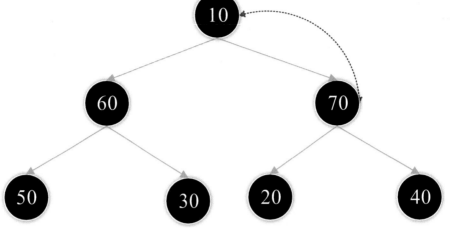

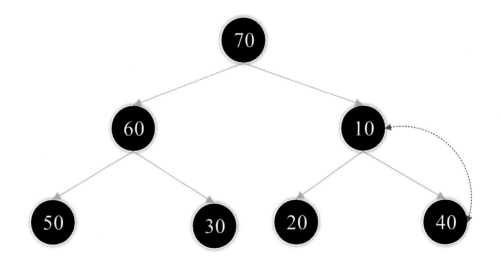

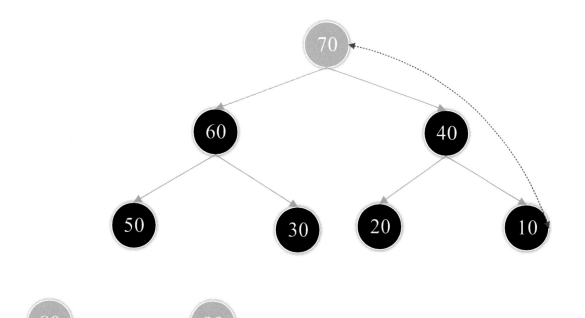

root = 70 and tail = 10 are exchanged

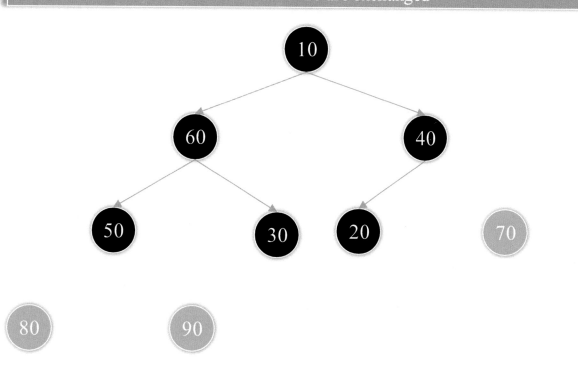

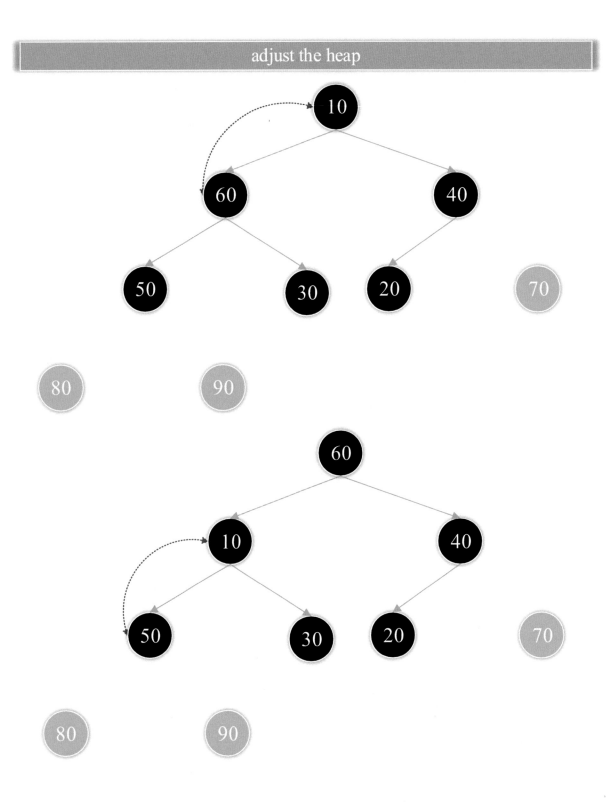

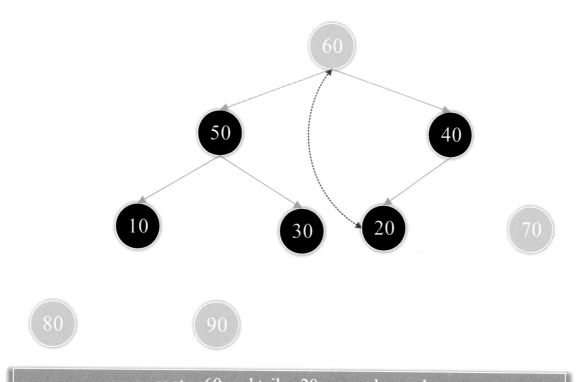

root = 60 and tail = 20 are exchanged

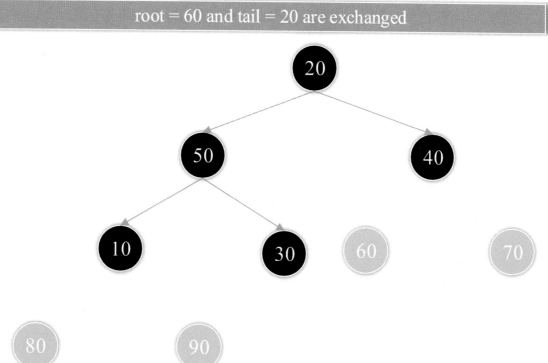

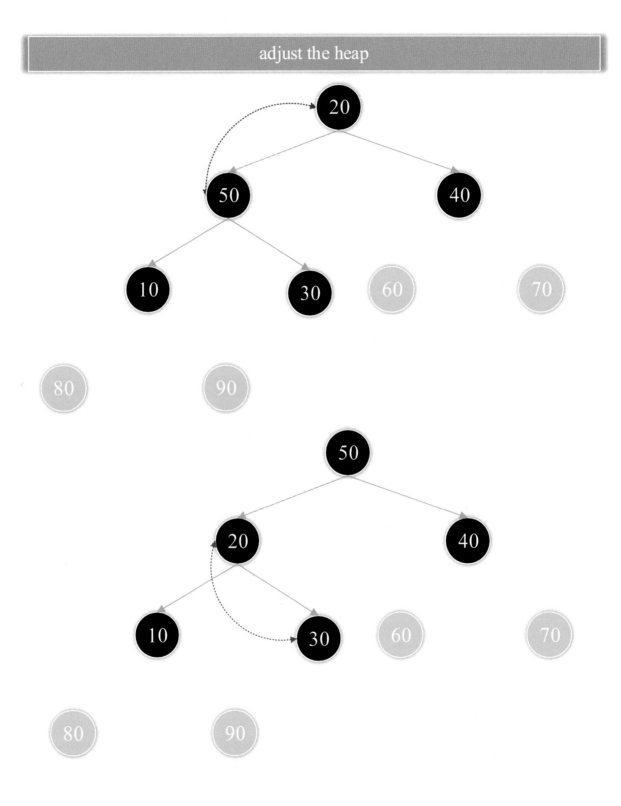

152

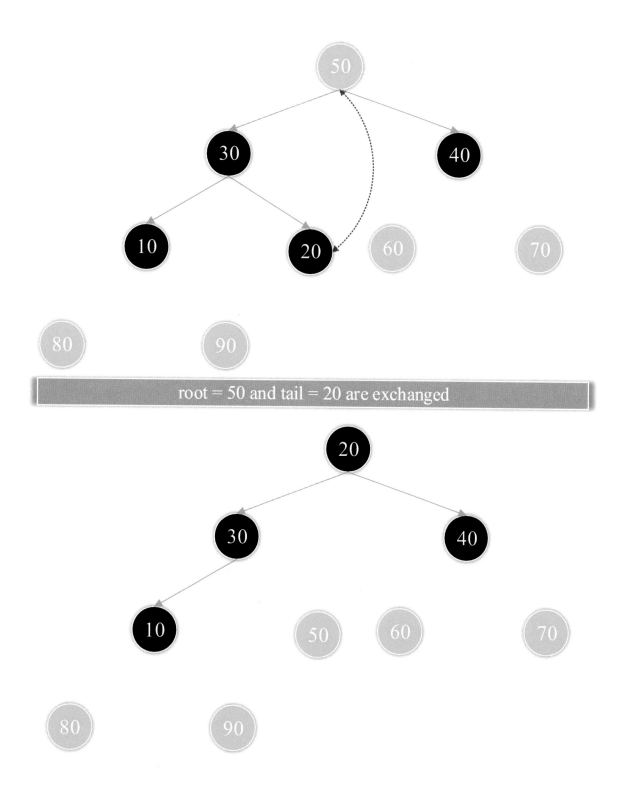

root = 50 and tail = 20 are exchanged

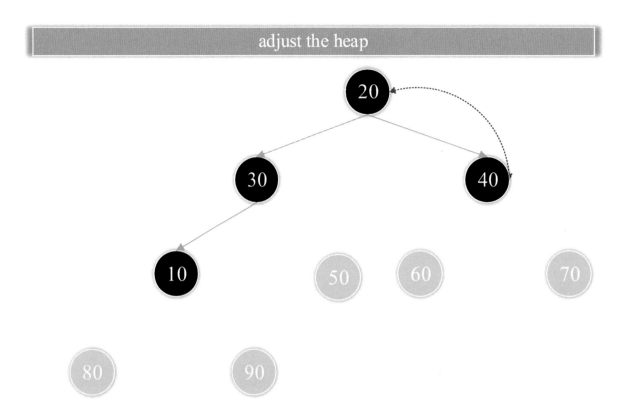

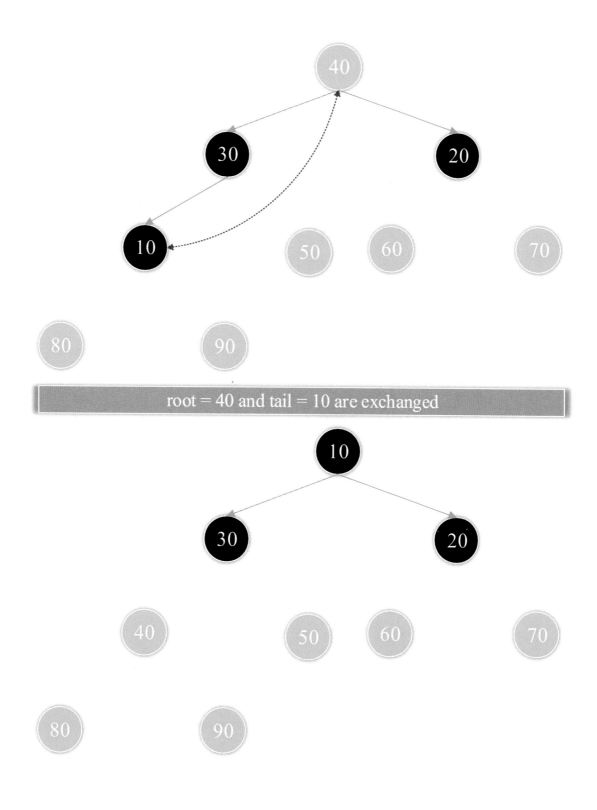

root = 40 and tail = 10 are exchanged

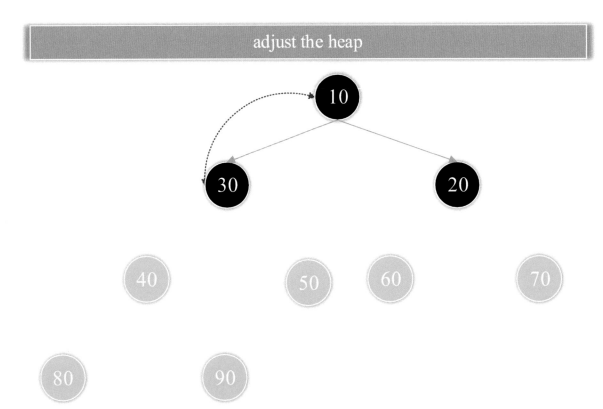

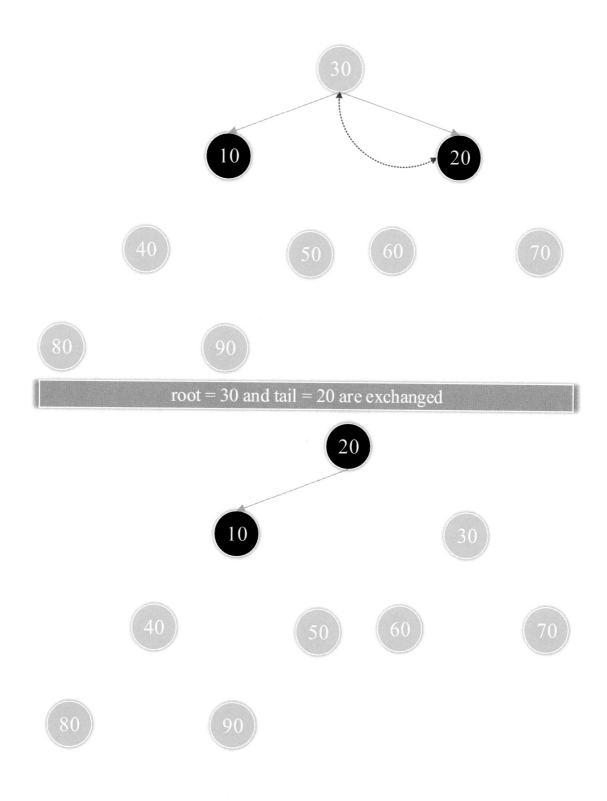

root = 30 and tail = 20 are exchanged

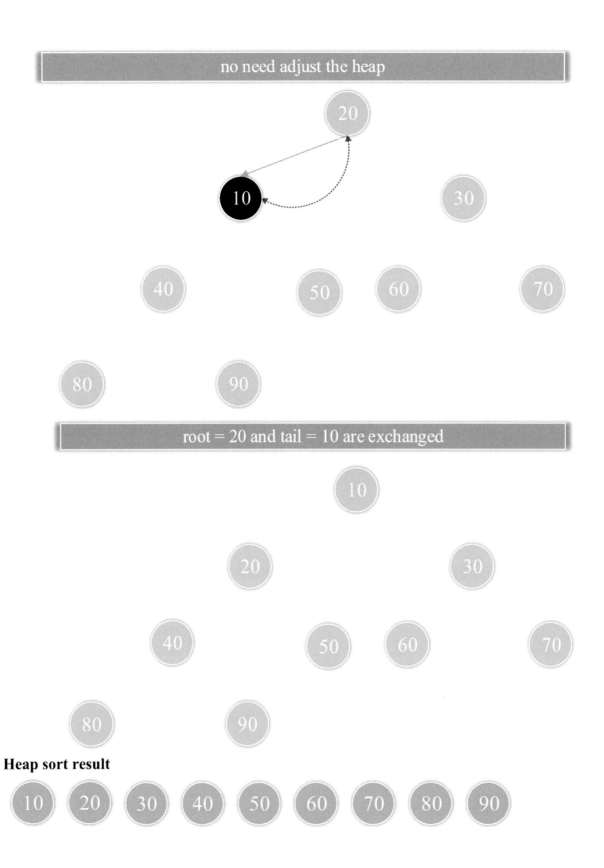

no need adjust the heap

root = 20 and tail = 10 are exchanged

Heap sort result

HeapSort.java

```java
public class HeapSort {
  private int[] array;

  public void createHeap(int[] array) {
    this.array = array;

    // Build a heap, (array.length - 1) / 2 scan half of the nodes with child nodes
    for (int i = (array.length - 1) / 2; i >= 0; i--) {
      adjustHeap(i, array.length - 1);
    }
  }

  public void adjustHeap(int currentIndex, int maxLength) {
    int noLeafValue = array[currentIndex]; // Current non-leaf node

    //2 * currentIndex + 1  Current left subtree subscript
    for (int j = 2 * currentIndex + 1; j <= maxLength; j = currentIndex * 2 + 1) {
      if (j < maxLength && array[j] < array[j + 1]) {
        j++; // j Large subscript
      }

      if (noLeafValue >= array[j]) {
        break;
      }

      array[currentIndex] = array[j]; // Move up to the parent node
      currentIndex = j;
    }

    array[currentIndex] = noLeafValue; // To put in the position
  }

  public void heapSort() {
    for (int i = array.length - 1; i > 0; i--) {
      int temp = array[0];
      array[0] = array[i];
      array[i] = temp;
      adjustHeap(0, i - 1);
    }
  }
}
```

TestHeapSort.java

```java
public class TestHeapSort {

    public static void main(String[] args) {
        HeapSort heapSort = new HeapSort();
        int[] scores = { 10, 90, 20, 80, 30, 70, 40, 60, 50 };

        System.out.println("Before building a heap : ");
        for (int i = 0; i < scores.length; i++) {
            System.out.print(scores[i] + ", ");
        }
        System.out.print("\n\n");

        System.out.println("After building a heap : ");
        heapSort.createHeap(scores);
        for (int i = 0; i < scores.length; i++) {
            System.out.print(scores[i] + ", ");
        }
        System.out.print("\n\n");

        System.out.println("After heap sorting : ");
        heapSort.heapSort();
        for (int i = 0; i < scores.length; i++) {
            System.out.print(scores[i] + ", ");
        }
    }
}
```

Result:
Before building a heap :
10 , 90 , 20 , 80 , 30 , 70 , 40 , 60 , 50 ,

After building a heap :
90 , 80 , 70 , 60 , 30 , 20 , 40 , 10 , 50 ,

After heap sorting :
10 , 20 , 30 , 40 , 50 , 60 , 70 , 80 , 90 ,

Hash Table

Hash Table:

A hash table is a data structure that is used to store keys/value pairs. It uses a hash function to compute an index into an array in which an element will be inserted or searched.

1. Map {19, 18, 35,40,41,42} to the HashTable mapping rule key % 4

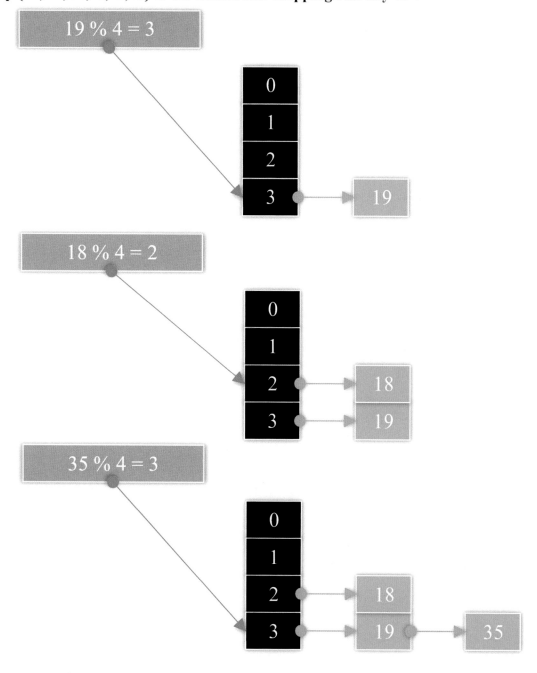

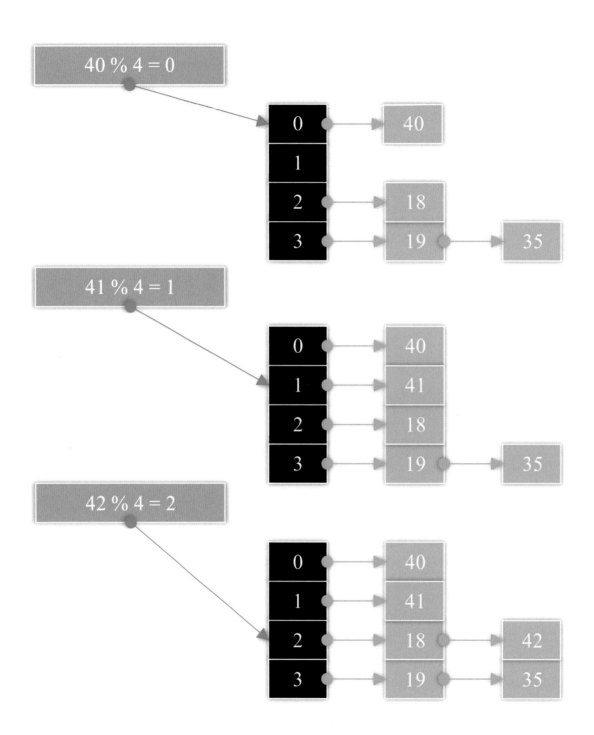

2. Implement a Hashtable

```
Node

-int hash
-Node next
-Object key
-Object value
-------------------------------------------
Node(Object key, Object value, int hash, Node next)
```

Node.java

```java
public class Node {
    private Object key;
    private Object value;
    private int hash;
    public Node next;

    public Node(Object key, Object value, int hash, Node next) {
        this.key = key;
        this.value = value;
        this.hash = hash;
        this.next = next;
    }

    public Object getKey() {
        return key;
    }
    public void setKey(String key) {
        this.key = key;
    }

    public Object getValue() {
        return value;
    }
    public void setValue(String value) {
        this.value = value;
    }

    public int getHash() {
        return hash;
    }
}
```

```java
    public void setHash(int hash) {
        this.hash = hash;
    }
}
```

Hashtable.java

```java
public class Hashtable {
    private Node[] table;
    private int capacity = 16;
    private int size;

    public Hashtable() {
        table = new Node[capacity];
    }

    //Initialize the Hashtable size
    public Hashtable(int capacity) {
        if (capacity < 0) {
            throw new IllegalArgumentException();
        } else {
            table = new Node[capacity];
            size = 0;
            this.capacity = capacity;
        }
    }

    public int size() {
        return size;
    }

    public boolean isEmpty() {
        return size == 0 ? true : false;
    }

    //Calculate the hash value according to the key hash algorithm
    private int hashCode(String key) {
        double avg = key.hashCode() * (Math.pow(5, 0.5) - 1) / 2; //hash policy for middle-
square method
        double numeric = avg - Math.floor(avg);
        return (int) Math.floor(numeric * capacity);
    }
```

```java
public void put(String key, String value) {
    if (key == null) {
        throw new IllegalArgumentException();
    }

    int hash = hashCode(key);
    Node newNode = new Node(key, value, hash, null);
    Node node = table[hash];
    while (node != null) {
        if (node.getKey().equals(key)) {
            node.setValue(value);
            return;
        }
        node = node.next;
    }

    newNode.next = table[hash];
    table[hash] = newNode;
    size++;
}

public Object get(String key) {
    if (key == null) {
        return null;
    }

    int hash = hashCode(key);
    Node node = table[hash];
    while (node != null) {//Get value according to key
        if (node.getKey().equals(key)) {
            return node.getValue();
        }
        node = node.next;
    }
    return null;
}
}
```

TestHashtable.java

```java
public class TestHashtable {

    public static void main(String[] args) {
        Hashtable table = new Hashtable();

        table.put("david", "Good Boy Keep Going");
        table.put("grace", "Cute Girl Keep Going");

        System.out.println("david => "+table.get("david"));
        System.out.println("grace => "+table.get("grace"));

    }

}
```

Result:
david => Good Boy Keep Going
grace => Cute Girl Keep Going

Directed Graph and Depth-First Search

Directed Graph:

The data structure is represented by an adjacency matrix (that is, a two-dimensional array) and an adjacency list. Each node is called a vertex, and two adjacent nodes are called edges.

Directed Graph has direction : A -> B and B -> A are different

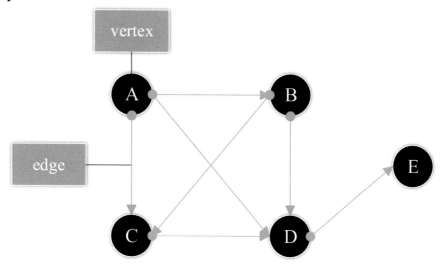

1. The adjacency matrix is described above:

The total number of vertices is a two-dimensional array size, if have value of the edge is 1, otherwise no value of the edge is 0.

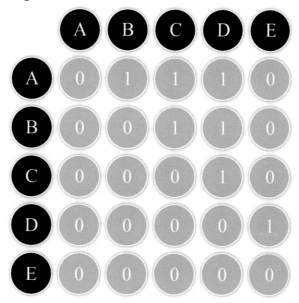

2. Depth-First Search:

Look for the neighboring edge node B from A and then find the neighboring node C from B and so on until all nodes are found A -> B -> C -> D -> E.

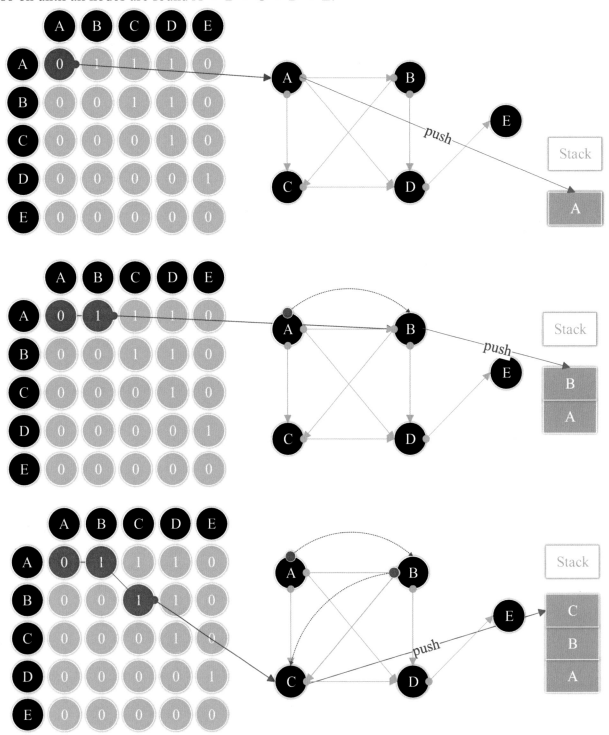

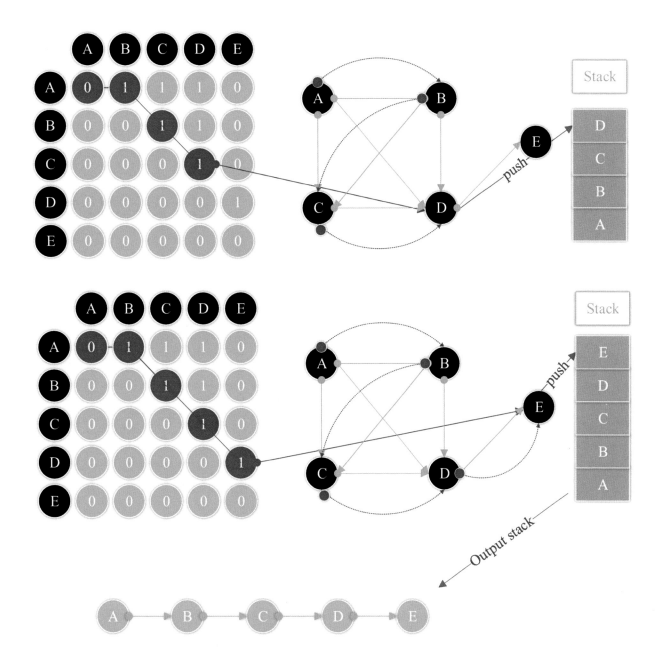

Vertex.java

```java
public class Vertex {

  private String data;
  private boolean visited; // Have you visited

  public Vertex() {
    super();
  }

  public Vertex(String data, boolean visited) {
    this.data = data;
    this.visited = visited;
  }

  public String getData() {
    return data;
  }

  public void setData(String data) {
    this.data = data;
  }

  public boolean isVisited() {
    return visited;
  }

  public void setVisited(boolean visited) {
    this.visited = visited;
  }

}
```

Graph.java

```java
import java.util.Stack;

public class Graph {
    private int maxVertexSize; // Two-dimensional array size
    private int size; // Current vertex size
    private Vertex[] vertexs;
    private int[][] adjacencyMatrix;

    private Stack<Integer> stack;// Stack saves current vertices

    public Graph(int maxVertexSize) {
        this.maxVertexSize = maxVertexSize;
        vertexs = new Vertex[maxVertexSize];

        adjacencyMatrix = new int[maxVertexSize][maxVertexSize];

        stack = new Stack<Integer>();
    }

    public void addVertex(String data) {
        Vertex vertex = new Vertex(data, false);
        vertexs[size] = vertex;
        size++;
    }

    // Add adjacent edges
    public void addEdge(int from, int to) {
        // A -> B  and B -> A are different
        adjacencyMatrix[from][to] = 1;
    }
```

```java
public void depthFirstSearch() {
    // Start searching from the first vertex
    Vertex firstVertex = vertexs[0];
    firstVertex.setVisited(true);
    System.out.print(firstVertex.getData());
    stack.push(0);

    while (!stack.isEmpty()) {
        int row = stack.peek();
        // Get adjacent vertex positions that have not been visited
        int col = findAdjacencyUnVisitedVertex(row);
        if (col == -1) {
            stack.pop();
        } else {
            vertexs[col].setVisited(true);
            System.out.print(" -> "+vertexs[col].getData());
            stack.push(col);
        }
    }

    clear();
}

// Get adjacent vertex positions that have not been visited
public int findAdjacencyUnVisitedVertex(int row) {
    for (int col = 0; col < size; col++) {
        if (adjacencyMatrix[row][col] == 1 && !vertexs[col].isVisited()) {
            return col;
        }
    }

    return -1;
}

// Clear reset
public void clear() {
    for (int i = 0; i < size; i++) {
        vertexs[i].setVisited(false);
    }
}
```

```java
    public int[][] getAdjacencyMatrix() {
        return adjacencyMatrix;
    }

    public Vertex[] getVertexs() {
        return vertexs;
    }

}
```

TestGraph.java

```java
public class TestGraph {

    public static void main(String[] args) {
        Graph graph = new Graph(5);
        graph.addVertex("A");
        graph.addVertex("B");
        graph.addVertex("C");
        graph.addVertex("D");
        graph.addVertex("E");

        graph.addEdge(0, 1);
        graph.addEdge(0, 2);
        graph.addEdge(0, 3);
        graph.addEdge(1, 2);
        graph.addEdge(1, 3);
        graph.addEdge(2, 3);
        graph.addEdge(3, 4);

        // Two-dimensional array traversal output vertex edge and adjacent array
        printGraph(graph);
        System.out.print("\nDepth-first search traversal output : \n");
        graph.depthFirstSearch();
    }
```

```
public static void printGraph(Graph graph) {
    System.out.print("output vertex edge and adjacent array :  \n   ");
    for (int i = 0; i < graph.getVertexs().length; i++) {
        System.out.print(graph.getVertexs()[i].getData() + "  ");
    }
    System.out.print("\n");

    for (int i = 0; i < graph.getAdjacencyMatrix().length; i++) {
        System.out.print(graph.getVertexs()[i].getData() + "  ");
        for (int j = 0; j < graph.getAdjacencyMatrix().length; j++) {
            System.out.print(graph.getAdjacencyMatrix()[i][j] + "  ");
        }
        System.out.print("\n");
    }
}
```

Result:

Two-dimensional array traversal output vertex edge and adjacent array :

```
   A   B   C   D   E
A  0   1   1   1   0
B  0   0   1   1   0
C  0   0   0   1   0
D  0   0   0   0   1
E  0   0   0   0   0
```

Depth-first search traversal output :
A -> B -> C -> D -> E

Directed Graph and Breadth-First Search

Directed Graph:

The data structure is represented by an adjacency matrix (that is, a two-dimensional array) and an adjacency list. Each node is called a vertex, and two adjacent nodes are called edges.

Directed Graph has direction : A -> B and B -> A are different

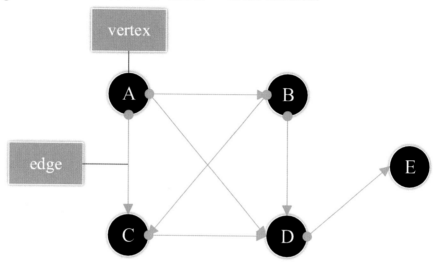

1. The adjacency matrix is described above:

The total number of vertices is a two-dimensional array size, if have value of the edge is 1, otherwise no value of the edge is 0.

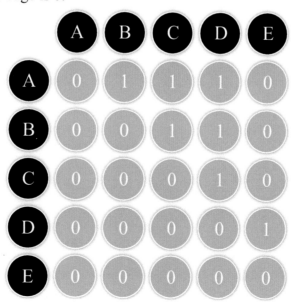

Breadth-First Search:

Find all neighboring edge nodes B, C, D from A and then find all neighboring nodes A, C, D from B and so on until all nodes are found A -> B -> C -> D -> E.

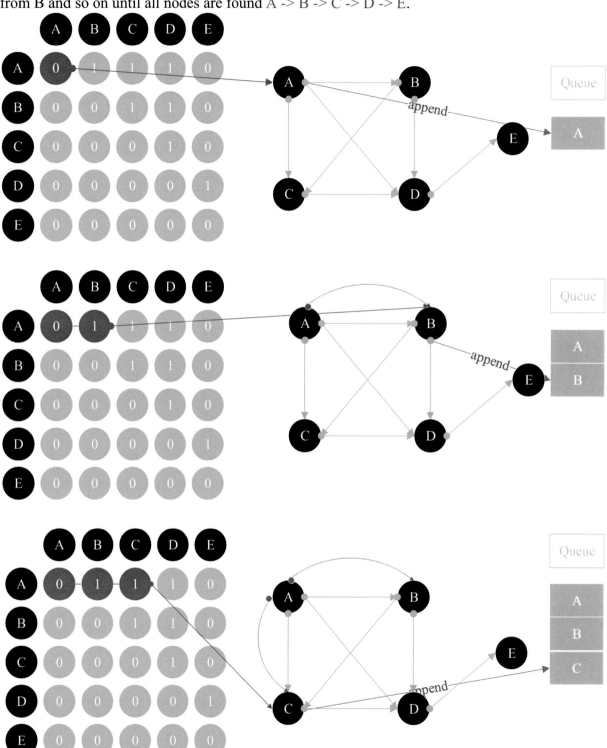

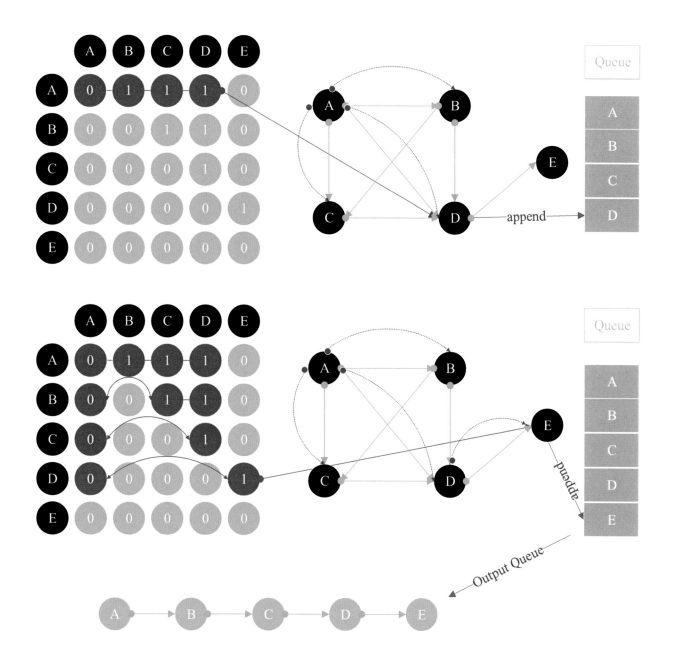

Vertex.java

```java
public class Vertex {

  private String data;
  private boolean visited; // Have you visited

  public Vertex() {
    super();
  }

  public Vertex(String data, boolean visited) {
    this.data = data;
    this.visited = visited;
  }

  public String getData() {
    return data;
  }

  public void setData(String data) {
    this.data = data;
  }

  public boolean isVisited() {
    return visited;
  }

  public void setVisited(boolean visited) {
    this.visited = visited;
  }

}
```

Graph.java

```java
import java.util.LinkedList;
import java.util.Queue;

public class Graph {
    private int maxVertexSize; // Two-dimensional array size
    private int size; // Current vertex size
    private Vertex[] vertexs;
    private int[][] adjacencyMatrix;
    private Queue<Integer> queue;// Queue saves current vertices

    public Graph(int maxVertexSize) {
        this.maxVertexSize = maxVertexSize;
        vertexs = new Vertex[maxVertexSize];
        adjacencyMatrix = new int[maxVertexSize][maxVertexSize];
        queue = new LinkedList<Integer>();
    }

    public void addVertex(String data) {
        Vertex vertex = new Vertex(data, false);
        vertexs[size] = vertex;
        size++;
    }

    // Add adjacent edges
    public void addEdge(int from, int to) {
    // A -> B  and B -> A are different
        adjacencyMatrix[from][to] = 1;
    }
```

```java
public void breadthFirstSearch() {
    // Start searching from the first vertex
    Vertex firstVertex = vertexs[0];
    firstVertex.setVisited(true);
    System.out.print(firstVertex.getData());
    queue.add(0);

    int col;
    while (!queue.isEmpty()) {
        int head = queue.remove();

        // Get adjacent vertex positions that have not been visited
        col = findAdjacencyUnVisitedVertex(head);

        //Loop through all vertices connected to the current vertex
        while (col != -1)
        {
            vertexs[col].setVisited(true);
            System.out.print(" -> "+vertexs[col].getData());
            queue.add(col);
            col = findAdjacencyUnVisitedVertex(head);
        }
    }
    clear();
}

// Get adjacent vertex positions that have not been visited
public int findAdjacencyUnVisitedVertex(int row) {
    for (int col = 0; col < size; col++) {
        if (adjacencyMatrix[row][col] == 1 && !vertexs[col].isVisited()) {
            return col;
        }
    }
    return -1;
}

// Clear reset
public void clear() {
    for (int i = 0; i < size; i++) {
        vertexs[i].setVisited(false);
    }
}
```

```java
    public int[][] getAdjacencyMatrix() {
        return adjacencyMatrix;
    }

    public Vertex[] getVertexs() {
        return vertexs;
    }

}
```

TestGraph.java

```java
public class TestGraph {

    public static void main(String[] args) {
        Graph graph = new Graph(5);

        graph.addVertex("A");
        graph.addVertex("B");
        graph.addVertex("C");
        graph.addVertex("D");
        graph.addVertex("E");

        graph.addEdge(0, 1);
        graph.addEdge(0, 2);
        graph.addEdge(0, 3);
        graph.addEdge(1, 2);
        graph.addEdge(1, 3);
        graph.addEdge(2, 3);
        graph.addEdge(3, 4);

        // Two-dimensional array traversal output vertex edge and adjacent array
        printGraph(graph);
        System.out.print("\nBreadth-First Search traversal output : \n");
        graph.breadthFirstSearch();
    }
```

```
public static void printGraph(Graph graph) {
    System.out.print("output vertex edge and adjacent array :  \n   ");
    for (int i = 0; i < graph.getVertexs().length; i++) {
        System.out.print(graph.getVertexs()[i].getData() + "  ");
    }
    System.out.print("\n");

    for (int i = 0; i < graph.getAdjacencyMatrix().length; i++) {
        System.out.print(graph.getVertexs()[i].getData() + "  ");
        for (int j = 0; j < graph.getAdjacencyMatrix().length; j++) {
            System.out.print(graph.getAdjacencyMatrix()[i][j] + "  ");
        }
        System.out.print("\n");
    }
}
```

Result:

Two-dimensional array traversal output vertex edge and adjacent array :

```
  A  B  C  D  E
A 0  1  1  1  0
B 0  0  1  1  0
C 0  0  0  1  0
D 0  0  0  0  1
E 0  0  0  0  0
```

Breadth-First Search traversal output :

A -> B -> C -> D -> E

Directed Graph Topological Sorting

Directed Graph Topological Sorting:
Sort the vertices in the directed graph with order of direction
.

Directed Graph has direction : A -> B and B -> A are different

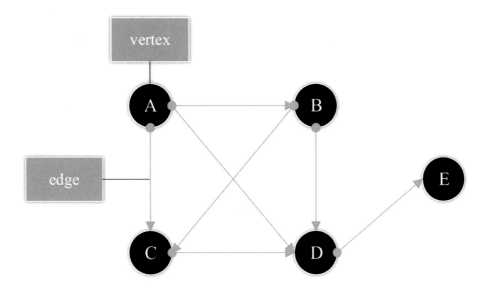

1. The adjacency matrix is described above:

The total number of vertices is a two-dimensional array size, if have value of the edge is 1, otherwise no value of the edge is 0.

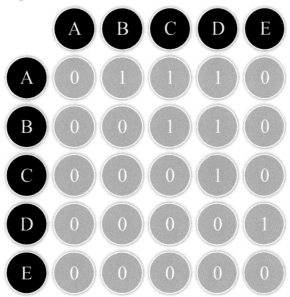

Topological sorting from vertex A : A -> B -> C -> D -> E

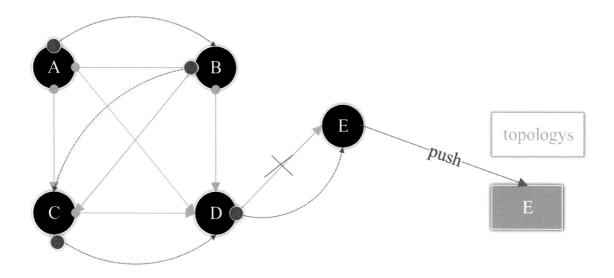

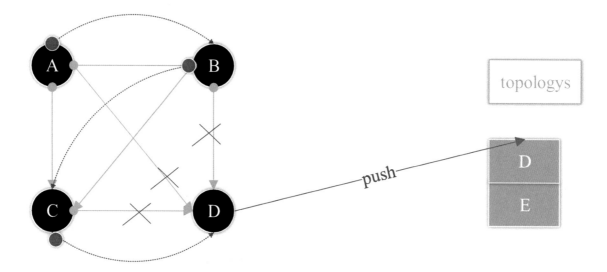

Find no successor vertices C then save to topologys, last C remove from the graph

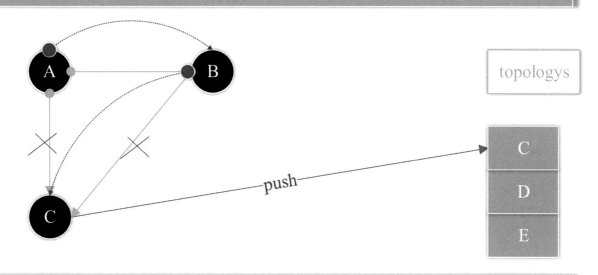

Find no successor vertices C then save to topologys, last C remove from the graph

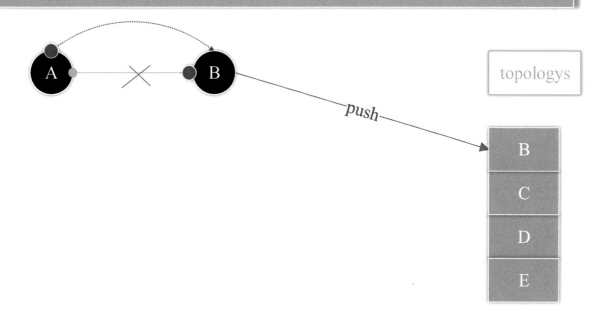

Find no successor vertices C then save to topologys, last C remove from the graph

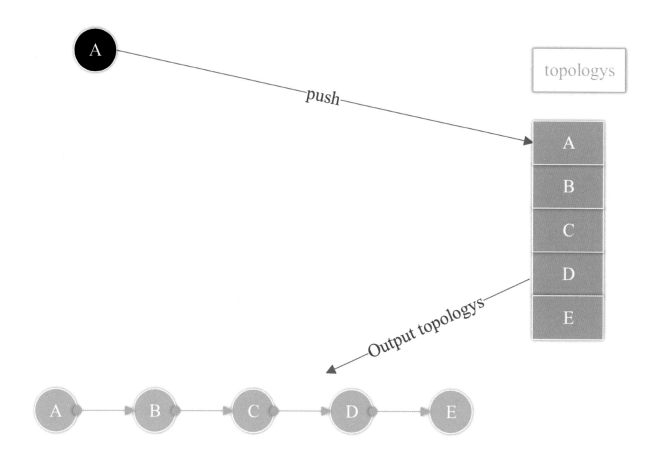

topologys

push

A
B
C
D
E

Output topologys

A → B → C → D → E

Vertex.java

```java
public class Vertex {

  private String data;
  private boolean visited; // Have you visited

  public Vertex() {
    super();
  }

  public Vertex(String data, boolean visited) {
    this.data = data;
    this.visited = visited;
  }

  public String getData() {
    return data;
  }

  public void setData(String data) {
    this.data = data;
  }

  public boolean isVisited() {
    return visited;
  }

  public void setVisited(boolean visited) {
    this.visited = visited;
  }

}
```

Graph.java

```java
public class Graph {
    private int maxVertexSize; // Two-dimensional array size
    private int size; // Current vertex size
    private Vertex[] vertexs;
    private int[][] adjacencyMatrix;

    // An array of topological sort results, recording the sorted sequence number of each node.
    private Vertex[] topologys;

    public Graph(int maxVertexSize) {
        this.maxVertexSize = maxVertexSize;
        vertexs = new Vertex[maxVertexSize];

        adjacencyMatrix = new int[maxVertexSize][maxVertexSize];

        topologys = new Vertex[maxVertexSize];
    }

    public void addVertex(String data) {
        Vertex vertex = new Vertex(data, false);
        vertexs[size] = vertex;
        size++;
    }

    // Add adjacent edges
    public void addEdge(int from, int to) {
        // A -> B  and B -> A are different
        adjacencyMatrix[from][to] = 1;
    }
```

```java
    public void topologySort() {
        while (size > 0) {
            int noSuccessorVertex = getNoSuccessorVertex();// Get a no successor node
            if (noSuccessorVertex == -1) {
                System.out.println("There is ring in Graph ");
                return;
            }
            topologys[size - 1] = vertexs[noSuccessorVertex];// Copy the deleted node to the
sorted array
            removeVertex(noSuccessorVertex);// Delete no successor node
        }
    }

    public int getNoSuccessorVertex() {
        boolean existSuccessor = false;
        for (int row = 0; row < size; row++) {// For each vertex
        existSuccessor = false;
        //If the node has a fixed row, each column has a 1, indicating that the node has a
successor, terminating the loop
            for (int col = 0; col < size; col++) {
                if (adjacencyMatrix[row][col] == 1) {
                    existSuccessor = true;
                    break;
                }
            }

            if (!existSuccessor) {// If the node has no successor, return its subscript
                return row;
            }
        }
        return -1;
    }
```

```java
public void removeVertex(int vertex) {
    if (vertex != size - 1) { //If the vertex is the last element, the end
        for (int i = vertex; i < size - 1; i++) {// The vertices are removed from the vertex array
            vertexs[i] = vertexs[i + 1];
        }

        for (int row = vertex; row < size - 1; row++) {// move up a row
            for (int col = 0; col < size - 1; col++) {
                adjacencyMatrix[row][col] = adjacencyMatrix[row + 1][col];
            }
        }

        for (int col = vertex; col < size - 1; col++) {// move left a row
            for (int row = 0; row < size - 1; row++) {
                adjacencyMatrix[row][col] = adjacencyMatrix[row][col + 1];
            }
        }
    }
    size--;// Decrease the number of vertices
}

public int[][] getAdjacencyMatrix() {
    return adjacencyMatrix;
}

public Vertex[] getVertexs() {
    return vertexs;
}

public Vertex[] getTopologys() {
    return topologys;
}

public int getSize() {
    return size;
}

}
```

TestGraph.java

```java
public class TestGraph {

  public static void main(String[] args) {
    Graph graph = new Graph(5);

    graph.addVertex("A");
    graph.addVertex("B");
    graph.addVertex("C");
    graph.addVertex("D");
    graph.addVertex("E");

    graph.addEdge(0, 1);
    graph.addEdge(0, 2);
    graph.addEdge(0, 3);
    graph.addEdge(1, 2);
    graph.addEdge(1, 3);
    graph.addEdge(2, 3);
    graph.addEdge(3, 4);

    // Two-dimensional array traversal output vertex edge and adjacent array
    printGraph(graph);

    System.out.print("\nDepth-First Search traversal output : \n");
    System.out.println("Directed Graph Topological Sorting:");
    graph.topologySort();
    for(int i=0;i< graph.getTopologys().length ; i++){
      System.out.print(graph.getTopologys()[i].getData()+" -> ");
    }
  }
}
```

```java
public static void printGraph(Graph graph) {
    System.out.print("traversal output vertex edge and adjacent array :  \n   ");
    for (int i = 0; i < graph.getVertexs().length; i++) {
        System.out.print(graph.getVertexs()[i].getData() + "  ");
    }
    System.out.print("\n");

    for (int i = 0; i < graph.getAdjacencyMatrix().length; i++) {
        System.out.print(graph.getVertexs()[i].getData() + "  ");
        for (int j = 0; j < graph.getAdjacencyMatrix().length; j++) {
            System.out.print(graph.getAdjacencyMatrix()[i][j] + "  ");
        }
        System.out.print("\n");
    }
}
```

Result:

Two-dimensional array traversal output vertex edge and adjacent array :

```
   A   B   C   D   E
A  0   1   1   1   0
B  0   0   1   1   0
C  0   0   0   1   0
D  0   0   0   0   1
E  0   0   0   0   0
```

Depth-First Search traversal output :
Directed Graph Topological Sorting:
A -> B -> C -> D -> E ->